Guide to God and Singularity

my perspective

Dr. Shravan Nanda

BlueRose ONE.com
Stories Matter
NewDelhi • London

BLUEROSE PUBLISHERS
India | U.K.

BlueRose ONE
Stories Matter
New Delhi • London

For permissions requests or inquiries regarding this publication, please contact:

BLUEROSE PUBLISHERS
www.BlueRoseONE.com
info@bluerosepublishers.com
+91 8882 898 898
+4407342408967

ISBN: 978-93-7018-536-4

Cover design: Yash Singhal
Typesetting: Namrata Saini

First Edition: September 2025

Preface

This is not a book.

It's a mirror.

A challenge.

A whisper across time.

I did not write this to tell you what God is. I wrote it to show you where the question leads.

In every temple, every tomb, every whispered prayer, and shouted truth—humans have been asking:

What exists before and after this existence?

I walked into that question with no scriptures in hand, only a strange knowing that everything must converge.

I saw the four sides—**Brahma, Vishnu, Shiva, and Shakti**—not as gods to be worshipped, but as **concepts too vast to ignore**. Each one a lens. Each one as a wall of a pyramid. Each belief system climbing upward, convinced it alone touches the truth.

But truth is not at the base. It is at the apex.

I did not lose myself in texts. I stepped back and saw the structure from above.

This book is a reflection of that view.

It is not an attempt to explain every religion, but to reveal the essence that every religion tries to explain.

It is the intersection of **ancient faith and future possibility**.

It is about **God**, not as an answer, but as a question that must evolve with us.

It is about **Singularity**—the moment when technology and human consciousness dissolve into one—and how our understanding of God must shift as we move toward it.

You may not agree with everything you read here. That is good.

Agreement is not the goal.

Awakening is.

Contents

Chapter 1
The Evolution of Human Understanding of God

Introduction: The Ultimate Question

What exists before or after this existence?

Picture yourself standing beneath an infinite sky. Stars glimmer like distant fires, stretching endlessly across the universe. The world is quiet, save for the gentle rustling of the grass and the crackling of a nearby fire. The warmth of the flames reaches you, and the distant echoes of unseen creatures in the darkness add an air of mystery.

Around the fire, a group of humans sit, staring upward in awe. Their minds grapple with the same question that has haunted humanity for millennia:

What was here before all this? Before the fire, before the stars, before life itself—what existed before existence, and what exists after?

This question is at the core of human spirituality. It has driven our ancestors to create myths, build temples, and meditate in search of meaning. Over time, various answers have emerged:

- **Some imagined a Creator**, a divine being who initiated the cosmos.

- **Others saw the universe itself as eternal**, self-sustaining, and divine.
- **Some pondered the concept of nothingness**; the void from which all things arise and to which they return.
- **Still others sensed a dynamic force**, an unseen energy that animates and connects all things.

These perspectives eventually developed into **four fundamental concepts of God**:

1. **Brahma (The Creator):** The divine initiator of existence.
2. **Vishnu (The Existence):** The universe as a living, divine entity.
3. **Shiva (Nothingness):** The nothingness from which creation emerges and returns.
4. **Shakti (The Energy):** The force that animates creation, sustenance, and dissolution.

This chapter takes you on a journey through human history, showing how these concepts emerged and evolved alongside the development of civilization. Together, they represent humanity's enduring search for truth and meaning.

1. The Dawn of Awareness: The First Sparks of Spirituality

(Time Period: c. 2.5 million BCE – 10,000 BCE, Palaeolithic Era)

The fire crackles and hisses, casting flickering shadows on the walls of the cave. Beyond the firelight, darkness swallows the surrounding forest. A flash of lightning briefly illuminates the landscape, followed by a deep rumble of thunder. The people sitting around the fire shudder.

In this moment, they are helpless before the forces of nature. Without knowledge of storms or seasons, they search for meaning in the world's unpredictable and terrifying events. They do what humans have always done—they imagine unseen powers that control these phenomena.

Is the sky angry? Has a spirit of the storm been provoked?

This is the world of early humans. It is a world full of mystery and danger, where survival is a daily struggle. Life and death hinge on forces they cannot see or control—forces they begin to interpret as **spirits.**

The Birth of Animism: Spirits in Nature

A hunter watches a deer move through the forest. To him, the deer is not just an animal—it is a **spiritual being**, imbued with life by the forest itself. When the hunter takes its life, he performs a ritual to thank the deer's spirit and ensure that the balance between life and death is maintained.

This belief in the spiritual nature of all things is known as **animism**. Early humans perceived **every aspect of nature** as alive and interconnected. Rivers, mountains, trees, and animals all have spirits. These spirits must be honoured to ensure harmony between humans and the natural world.

Over time, **shamans** emerge as spiritual guides. They claim to communicate with the spirits through visions, rituals, and trances. The community looks to them for guidance, protection, and healing.

Across different continents, animistic beliefs take shape:

- **In Africa**, tribes honour the spirits of ancestors and the land.
- **In Australia**, Aboriginal peoples tell **Dreamtime stories**, which describe the creation of the world by ancestral beings.
- **In the America**, Native tribes revere the **Great Spirit**, present in all living things.

How This Shaped the Concept of God

- **Vishnu's presence:** The world itself is seen as sacred, reflecting the divine presence in all things.

Transition: As humans discover agriculture and settle into villages, their relationship with the divine changes. **Gods of stability and abundance replace the spirits of survival.**

2. The Agricultural Revolution: Stability, Gods, and Rituals

(Time Period: c. 10,000 BCE – 3,000 BCE, Neolithic Era)

You now stand at the edge of a flourishing village. Fields of crops stretch out before you, swaying gently in the wind. **Golden wheat**, **tall maize**, and **flooded rice paddies** shimmer under the sun. Farmers work tirelessly, their hands planting, watering, and harvesting the crops that sustain their community.

This is the dawn of agriculture. Humans have learned to manipulate the earth—**planting seeds**, **irrigating fields**, and **domesticating animals**. Yet, despite these advancements, nature remains unpredictable. **What if the rains do not come? What if disease strikes the crops?**

In response to this uncertainty, humans turn to **gods of agriculture** who govern the cycles of planting and harvest.

The Rise of Agricultural Deities

Farming follows **cyclical patterns**—birth, growth, death, and renewal. These patterns inspire new gods who embody the forces of fertility, weather, and abundance. Temples and altars are built to honour these deities, and festivals mark key moments in the agricultural cycle.

- In **Mesopotamia**, **Enlil** (god of wind) and **Inanna** (goddess of fertility) are worshipped through offerings and rituals performed on towering ziggurats.
- In **Egypt**, the Nile's flood is seen as a gift from **Hapi**, the river god, while **Ra**, the sun god, sustains all life.
- In **India**, the earliest stages of **Vedic Hinduism** mirrored this pattern. The **Rigveda**, composed around this time, contained hymns honouring deities such as **Agni** (fire), **Indra** (storm), and **Soma** (a sacred plant), whose blessings were seen as essential for agricultural success.

Priests become spiritual authorities, tasked with performing the rituals that ensure the land's fertility and prosperity. Religion is no longer just about survival—it becomes **a cornerstone of social order**.

How This Shaped the Concept of God

- **Brahma's concept solidifies:** Creation and cosmic order are attributed to powerful deities.
- **Vishnu's influence grows:** The cycles of nature reflect divine sustenance.

- **Shakti manifests:** Rituals are seen as channels for divine energy, guiding the fate of crops and communities.

3. The Rise of Civilizations: Religion Becomes Law

(Time Period: c. 3,000 BCE – 500 BCE)

The streets of a great city hum with life. Merchants shout to customers, offering goods from distant lands. Priests perform ceremonies in towering temples, while scribes carve laws into stone tablets. Religion has become intertwined with **law, governance, and morality**, shaping the very structure of society.

In this era, rulers claim **divine authority**, often portrayed as intermediaries between gods and humans. Religion serves as both a **spiritual guide** and a **means of control**, ensuring societal stability through divine laws.

Codification of Belief Systems

With the development of writing, religious ideas are recorded for the first time, solidifying doctrines and rituals for future generations. Sacred texts become the foundation of religious practice and law:

- **In Mesopotamia**, the **Code of Hammurabi** declares that laws are divinely inspired: "An eye for an eye, a tooth for a tooth."
- **In Egypt**, the concept of **Ma'at** (cosmic order) governs both the natural world and human behaviour. Pharaohs are seen as living gods tasked with maintaining this balance.

- In **India**, Vedic religious practices begin evolving into **Brahmanism**, characterized by intricate rituals aimed at sustaining both social and cosmic order. The **Yajurveda** and **Atharvaveda** elaborated on sacrificial rites, while priests maintained control over religious authority. Over time, dissatisfaction with ritualism give rise to a more introspective spiritual movement—**the Upanishads**.
- **In Israel**, **Moses** delivers the **Torah**, which defines a covenant between the Jewish people and their God. God is seen as one creator, separated from creation.
- **In Persia**, **Zoroaster** teaches about the eternal struggle between **Ahura Mazda** (the god of truth) and **Angra Mainyu** (the spirit of evil).

These codified systems shape not only religious life but also governance, law, and cultural identity.

How This Shaped the Concept of God

- **Brahma's prominence:** Creation and cosmic authority are embodied in divine laws and rulers. God is seen as a creator who brought creation into existence.
- **Vishnu's influence deepens:** Sustenance of the social and natural order is seen as part of divine will.
- **Shiva's idea emerges:** Early ideas of **Shiva** begin to crystallize. Although Vedic texts emphasized gods like **Agni** and **Indra**, the need for a deeper understanding of **dissolution and transcendence** becomes apparent. The seeds of Shiva's concept—as both a destroyer and a force of renewal—would later

flourish in **Shaivism**, representing the natural cycle of creation, sustenance, and destruction.

- **Shakti's energy:** Rituals and festivals maintain cosmic harmony by channeling divine power.

Transition: As civilizations expand and connect through trade and conquest, a new wave of thought emerges—one that emphasizes **ethics, introspection, and the search for universal truths**.

4. The Axial Age: The Birth of Philosophy and Monotheism

(Time Period: 800 BCE – 200 BCE)

You find yourself in a marketplace in **Athens**, surrounded by philosophers debating the nature of existence. A man named **Socrates** questions the crowd:

"What is justice? What is truth? How should one live?"

This intellectual curiosity is not unique to Greece. Across the world, people are beginning to ask **profound questions** about life, death, and the divine. This period, known as the **Axial Age**, marks a turning point in human thought.

A Global Awakening

During the Axial Age, philosophers and spiritual leaders across cultures began to explore the **nature of existence and the cycle of life and death**. This era saw the emergence of **philosophical Hinduism**. The **Upanishads** emphasized the idea of **Atman** (the eternal self), which transcends the cycle of birth and death. Shiva, as a symbol of dissolution, reflected the **impermanence of worldly attachments** and the path to ultimate liberation (**moksha**).

During this time, new religious and philosophical systems arise, each emphasizing **morality, self-awareness, and cosmic order**:

- **In India**, **Siddhartha Gautama** (the Buddha) teaches that enlightenment comes through understanding and overcoming suffering. The **Upanishads** transformed Hindu thought, moving beyond ritual to explore the nature of **Atman** (the self) and **Brahman** (the ultimate reality). Concepts like **karma**, **samsara**, and **moksha** redefined the human relationship with the cosmos, emphasizing self-realization as the path to liberation.
- **In China**, **Confucius** emphasizes social harmony and ethical behaviour, while **Laozi** speaks of the **Tao**—the natural flow of the universe.
- **In Persia**, **Zoroaster** promotes dualism, the struggle between good and evil, urging people to align with **truth** and **righteousness**.
- **In Israel**, Jewish prophets refine monotheism, asserting that there is one God who demands justice and compassion.
- **In Greece**, philosophers like **Plato** and **Aristotle** explore reason, ethics, and the nature of the soul.

This era introduces **philosophical religions** and **ethical monotheism**, reshaping humanity's relationship with the divine.

The Rise of Monotheism

One of the most significant shifts during the Axial Age is the rise of **monotheism**—the belief in a single, all-powerful God. In **Judaism**, God is seen as the Creator and Sustainer of the universe, who enters into a covenant with His people. This idea influences the later development of **Christianity** and **Islam**, which spread monotheism across much of the world.

How This Shaped the Concept of God:

- **Brahma gains new clarity:** God is seen as both the Creator and moral authority.
- **Vishnu's presence persists:** The divine sustains existence and interacts with humanity.
- **Shivas importance in cyclical nature: Shiva** becomes central to the concept of **cyclical time** and **transcendence. Idea of nothingness emerges!**
- **Shakti remains implicit:** Divine energy is expressed through spiritual transformation and moral action.

Transition: With the spread of these ideas, religions become **global** in scope, transcending cultural boundaries and shaping civilizations across continents.

5. Universal Religions and Global Expansion

(Time Period: 1st Century CE – 15th Century CE)

Religions now begin to take on **universal aspirations**, spreading far beyond their places of origin:

- **Christianity**, originating in the Middle East, spreads across the Roman Empire and beyond, emphasizing salvation through faith in Jesus Christ.
- **Islam**, founded in the Arabian Peninsula, expands rapidly across the Middle East, Africa, and Asia, uniting diverse peoples under the concept of **Tawhid** (the oneness of God).
- **Buddhism** travels along the **Silk Road**, reaching China, Korea, Japan, and Southeast Asia, adapting to local cultures while maintaining its core teachings.

Hinduism's Evolution: The Rise of Philosophical Schools and Reformers

While Christianity, Islam, and Buddhism expanded across continents, **Hinduism in India took a different path—one of continuous evolution and reinterpretation.** Unlike many religions with fixed doctrines, Hinduism has always been dynamic, shaped by new ideas, philosophical debates, and spiritual reformers.

During this period, **great thinkers and scholars emerge**, refining and reshaping Hindu thought. Four of the most influential among them were:

1. **Adi Shankaracharya (Advaita Vedanta – Non-Dualism)**
    - Shankaracharya (8th century CE) revived **Advaita Vedanta**, a school of thought that asserts **there is only one ultimate reality—Brahman—and everything else is an illusion (Maya).**
    - He argued that **the soul (Atman) and Brahman (the universal consciousness) are one and the**

same, emphasizing the idea of unity beyond all dualities.

   - His teachings reinforced **the concept of Vishnu as all-pervading consciousness** and **Shiva as the unchanging absolute reality.**

2. **Ramanujacharya (Vishishtadvaita – Qualified Non-Dualism)**
   - Ramanuja (11th–12th century CE) challenged Shankaracharya's pure non-dualism, proposing **a middle ground** where the **soul is distinct from Brahman but still connected to it.**
   - He emphasized **devotion (Bhakti) to Vishnu as the path to liberation**, making **Vaishnavism a deeply personal and devotional movement.**
   - His philosophy influenced Bhakti traditions across India, reinforcing **Vishnu's concept as both the universe and its guiding force.**

3. **Madhvacharya (Dvaita – Dualism)**
   - Madhvacharya (13th century CE) took a radically different approach, proposing **Dvaita Vedanta (Dualism), where God (Vishnu) and the soul are eternally separate.**
   - He argued that **liberation comes through unwavering devotion to Vishnu as a distinct, supreme being.**
   - His teachings laid the foundation for **many modern Vaishnavite traditions, particularly in Southern India.**

4. **Nimbarkacharya (Dvaitadvaita – Duality in Unity)**
    - Nimbarka (12th century CE) introduced **Dvaitadvaita (Dualistic Non-Dualism), combining both Shankara's non-dualism and Madhva's dualism.**
    - He taught that **souls and the universe are distinct from God (Krishna/Vishnu) yet also inseparably dependent on Him.**
    - His teachings reinforced **Bhakti (devotion) as the means to experiencing the divine.**

These religions establish **hierarchies**, **canonical texts**, and **missionary efforts** to sustain their growth. They also engage in **inter-religious dialogue** and **conflict**, shaping the spiritual and political landscape of the medieval world.

Transition: As the modern world emerges, religions face new challenges from science, secularism, and globalization.

6. The Reformation, Enlightenment, and the Changing Face of God

The **16th to 19th centuries** were marked by **major shifts in religious thought**. The **Protestant Reformation** shattered the dominance of the Catholic Church in Europe, emphasizing **personal interpretation of scripture over institutional authority**. The **Enlightenment** further challenged religious orthodoxy, promoting **reason, scientific inquiry, and skepticism of dogma**.

Meanwhile, **colonialism** spread Christianity and Islam to new regions, often forcefully displacing indigenous spiritual traditions. Yet, paradoxically, this also led to greater

religious pluralism, as ideas and beliefs from different cultures encountered one another, reshaping theological perspectives.

Diverse Interpretations of God in Abrahamic Faiths

As these transformations unfolded, **new interpretations of God emerged within Christianity, Judaism, and Islam**. These interpretations reflected both **faith and reason**, as religious scholars and thinkers attempted to reconcile the divine with new understandings of the universe.

1. Christianity: From a Distant Creator to an Immanent Presence

- The Reformation rejected the idea that divine authority was controlled by the Church, shifting focus to **personal faith and direct connection with God**.
- Some Protestant traditions moved toward a **deistic** view—God as the **Creator** who set the universe into motion but does not interfere (**Brahma's concept**).
- Others, influenced by mystical traditions, emphasized **God's presence within all things**—a shift toward **panentheism** (**Vishnu's concept**).

2. Judaism: The Struggle Between Tradition and Modernity

- Jewish philosophers like Baruch Spinoza challenged traditional monotheism, arguing that God and nature are one and the same, leading to a pantheistic interpretation of the divine (Vishnu's concept).

- Meanwhile, **Hasidic Judaism** emphasized **God's immanence in everyday life**, promoting a more mystical, personal relationship with the divine.

3. Islam: Rationalism and Mysticism Emerge

- Islamic philosophers like Averroes (Ibn Rushd) and Al-Farabi embraced reason and attempted to harmonize faith with Aristotelian philosophy, suggesting a God who governs the universe through natural laws rather than direct intervention (Brahma's concept).
- Sufism, on the other hand, expanded the mystical understanding of God, emphasizing oneness with the divine through spiritual practices (Vishnu's concept).

Hinduism's Response: The Rise of New Thinkers and Reformers

While the Western world was grappling with **scientific revolution and religious reform**, **Hinduism underwent its own period of philosophical and social transformation**. New Hindu thinkers and reformers emerged, reshaping Hindu theology, ethics, and spirituality in response to colonialism, modernity, and scientific progress.

1. Chaitanya Mahaprabhu (15th–16th Century CE) – Bhakti as the Path to God

- Chaitanya was a key proponent of the **Bhakti movement**, emphasizing **devotional love for Krishna**.
- His teachings aligned with **Vishnu's concept**, promoting **a personal connection to God rather than ritualistic practices.**
- His influence led to **Gaudiya Vaishnavism**, which later inspired movements like ISKCON.

2. Swami Vivekananda (19th Century CE) – Hinduism and Science

- A disciple of Ramakrishna, Vivekananda bridged Hindu philosophy with modern scientific thinking.
- He introduced Advaita Vedanta (non-dualism) to the West, asserting that God is not separate from existence but rather its very essence (Vishnu's concept).
- His famous speech at the Parliament of World Religions in 1893 promoted religious unity, tolerance, and the idea of an all-pervading divine presence.

3. Raja Ram Mohan Roy (18th–19th Century CE) – The Brahmo Samaj Movement

- A reformer who challenged idol worship and promoted a monotheistic interpretation of Hinduism, aligning with Brahma's concept.
- He sought to remove superstition, caste discrimination, and outdated traditions, making Hinduism more rational and ethical.
- His ideas helped lay the foundation for modern Hindu reform movements.

4. Sri Aurobindo (19th–20th Century CE) – The Evolution of Consciousness

- Aurobindo integrated Hindu spirituality with modern science, proposing that human consciousness is evolving toward a higher divine state (Shakti's concept).
- His Integral Yoga philosophy emphasized the transformation of human life through divine energy (Shakti), rather than renunciation.

How This Shaped the Concept of God

These shifts had massive effects on humanity's perception of God:

- **Brahma (the Creator) faces challenges**:
  - Scientific advancements, including **theories of evolution and the Big Bang, undermine the**

necessity of a divine Creator in explaining existence.

  - Deism and rationalist interpretations **reduce God's role to an initial creator who does not intervene in human affairs**.
- **Vishnu (the Divine Universe) adapts:**
  - **Pantheism and panentheism** gain traction, suggesting that **God is not separate from the universe but within it**.
  - Hindu reformers like **Swami Vivekananda** reinforce this idea by **merging Advaita Vedanta with scientific rationalism.**
- **Shiva (the Void) gains scientific validation:**
  - **Atheism and existentialism** align with **Shiva's concept**, proposing that **there is no divine being—only the vast nothingness of the cosmos**.
  - The idea that **life has no inherent meaning unless humans create it** echoes **Shiva's role as both dissolution and transformation**.
- **Shakti (the Energy of Transformation) re-emerges:**
  - Mysticism, Sufism, and Kabbalah **emphasize divine energy as a force beyond form or dogma**.
  - Theories of **vital force, consciousness, and interconnected energy fields** emerge, mirroring Shakti's **dynamic, all-pervading power**.

- Sri Aurobindo's **Integral Yoga** presents **Shakti as an evolutionary force driving human consciousness forward.**

Transition: The Birth of a Global Spiritual Consciousness

As the modern era unfolds, these ideas continue to evolve. With the rise of **globalization, technology, and scientific breakthroughs**, spirituality is no longer confined to cultural boundaries. **The 20th and 21st centuries mark the emergence of a more interconnected religious landscape, where traditions blend, new philosophies arise, and the search for God takes on new forms.**

This leads us into the **Contemporary Era—where religion, science, and philosophy converge like never before.**

7. The Contemporary Era: Globalization and Spiritual Diversification

(Time Period: 20th Century CE – Present)

In today's world, religion is both more diverse and more interconnected than ever before. **Globalization** has facilitated **interfaith dialogue**, while technology allows people to explore spiritual traditions from across the globe.

New religious movements, such as **New Age spirituality** and **mindfulness practices**, reflect modern humanity's evolving spiritual needs. At the same time, **secularism** and **atheism** challenge traditional religious frameworks.

The evolution of religion mirrors humanity's intellectual and cultural growth. From animism to monotheism, from ritual to philosophy, religion has adapted to address humanity's deepest questions.

But just as this journey is universal, it is also deeply personal. In the next chapter, I will share my own story of faith, doubt, and discovery—a journey that led me to realize the timeless truth of the four concepts of God.

Chapter 2
My Journey of Realization

Introduction: A Personal Search for the Divine

Understanding the divine is not merely a theological exercise—it is deeply personal. My journey began with the faith I was born into, evolved through challenges that reshaped my worldview, and culminated in a profound realization: the universal understanding of God can be interpreted through four fundamental concepts.

If Chapter 1 traced humanity's collective journey toward spiritual understanding, this chapter delves into my own story—a reflection of that larger journey. It is a story of **belief**, **doubt**, **exploration**, and **synthesis**. It is about moving beyond inherited faith to arrive at a broader, more interconnected understanding of the divine.

Through the trials of life and the existential questions they provoked, I discovered not just new spiritual truths, but also a **vision for humanity's path forward**—a vision shaped by the search for **singularity** and the desire to **overcome duality** in human existence.

Faith in the Beginning: The Foundation of Vaishnavism

I was born into a **Vaishnavite family**, where Vishnu was revered as the **sustainer of the universe**. Vishnu, as I understood Him in my childhood, was not only the preserver of existence but the **essence of existence itself**—an eternal, all-encompassing force.

My earliest memories are intertwined with **rituals, festivals**, and the warmth of **community gatherings**. My grandfather, **Ramakrishna Gowder**, a deeply devout man, had built a temple dedicated to **Lakshmi Narasimha Swamy**, a fierce yet protective form of Vishnu with his consort Lakshmi. This temple was more than a place of worship; it was a **sanctuary for spiritual connection**.

The rhythmic chants of **Shantakaram Bhujagashayanam**, describing Vishnu reclining on the serpent **Ananta**, echoed through the temple during prayers. For me, this image symbolized **serenity amidst chaos** and the **infinite balance** between power and peace. I recited these shlokas daily with my mother during my morning prayers, finding comfort in the belief that Vishnu was ever-present, **sustaining the world** around me.

Festivals like **Vishu, Ugadi, and Deepavali** were integral to our lives, celebrating Vishnu's role as both **protector** and **embodiment of righteousness**. My family taught me that faith in Vishnu was a path to **peace** and **purpose**, and for many years, this belief formed the foundation of my spiritual identity.

Yet, even in those early days, questions lingered at the edges of my consciousness:

- **What lies beyond creation?**
- **If Vishnu sustains existence, what sustains Him?**

These questions, though dormant, would later resurface and challenge my understanding of the divine.

The Crisis of Faith: A Turning Point in Ukraine

Life has a way of testing even the strongest beliefs. During my medical studies in Ukraine, I faced a period of intense personal and familial turmoil. I prayed fervently to Vishnu, seeking **guidance** and **resolution**, but my prayers seemed unanswered. This silence left me questioning the foundation of my faith:

- **Had I misunderstood Vishnu's role?**
- **Was my belief simply a product of my upbringing?**
- **Why would the sustainer of the universe allow such chaos to persist?**

Exploring Christianity: An Encounter with the Creator

At the height of my crisis, a close Christian friend in Ukraine suggested I explore his faith. According to him, the Christian God was the **true Creator** of the universe—the source of all truth. Though I had been exposed to Christianity in my early life, this time I approached it with a more open mind.

I began reading the **Bible**, particularly the **Book of Genesis**, which captivated me with its portrayal of **God as the architect of creation**. The imagery of God separating

light from darkness and bringing order to the universe resonated with my need for clarity amidst the chaos in my life.

Christianity's emphasis on **salvation** through **Jesus Christ** introduced me to the idea of God as both **Creator** and **Redeemer**. The concept of the **Incarnation**—God becoming human to share in humanity's struggles—was deeply moving. For a time, I believed I had found the answers I was seeking.

At this point, **life events began to shift**. I started to notice subtle improvements in my situation—challenges began resolving, and I found myself more grounded. For the moment, I did not dwell on whether these changes were coincidences or **divine intervention**. Instead, I chose to **go with the flow**, allowing the unfolding of events to guide me forward.

However, this phase of relative peace soon led to a deeper spiritual challenge when I encountered new perspectives on God. These interactions marked a **pivotal moment** in my journey.

Islam and the Question That Shattered My Belief

Around this time, I met a friend from Libya, a devout Muslim, who shared his perspective on the nature of God. When I expressed my belief that **Jesus might be God**, he posed a simple but profound question:

"How can a human be God? Isn't Jesus a creation, not the Creator?"

This question shattered my newly formed beliefs, forcing me to confront the **distinction between Creator and creation**. In Islam, **Allah** is presented as the **ultimate Creator**, eternal and beyond human comprehension. I began studying the **Quran** and the concept of **Tawhid**—the absolute oneness of God.

Allah was portrayed as **all-powerful** and **all-knowing**. But this brought me face-to-face with another paradox:

If God is all-knowing and has predetermined every event, where does human free will fit in?

The more I pondered this question, the more I struggled to reconcile the idea of **predetermination** with genuine **freedom of choice**. How could human actions be truly free if God already knew and ordained every outcome? This question left me at a deadlock.

No matter how deeply I explored Islamic theology, the tension between **omniscience** (state of knowing everything) and **free will** (ability to **make your own choices** without being completely controlled by fate, destiny, or external forces) remained unresolved. I kept asking questions—discussing these ideas with scholars and believers—but each answer seemed to circle back to the idea that **God's will was absolute**. Free will, in this framework, appeared illusory.

These unresolved questions ultimately pushed me to seek answers beyond the boundaries of Islam, guiding me back to **Hinduism**, where I would encounter new ways of thinking about **creation, existence, and the self**.

Returning to Vaishnavism: A New Understanding of Free Will

When I returned to **Vaishnavism**, I found myself approaching its teachings with renewed curiosity and openness. Hindu philosophy offered multiple perspectives on **creation**, **sustenance**, and **dissolution**, but it also introduced concepts that spoke directly to my struggle with free will and divine knowledge.

In **Hinduism**, the universe is seen not as a rigid, predetermined system, but as a dynamic interplay of forces governed by **karma (past)** and **dharma (future)**. **Karma**—the law of cause and effect—allows for both divine order and human agency.

Karma is the **path behind you**, shaped by your past actions and their effects on your present life. It creates challenges or opportunities based on what you have done before. However, you can change your future by learning from these experiences and making better choices now.

Dharma is the **path ahead**, guiding you toward a purposeful and balanced life through right actions. It shows you how to make decisions that align with truth and harmony. By following dharma, you can move beyond old patterns and shape a better future.

The **present** is where **karma** and **dharma** meet, offering you the chance to grow. Your past actions affect your current reality, but your present choices create your future. By choosing actions aligned with dharma, you can free yourself from limitations and move closer to spiritual freedom and unity.

In this view, humans are **co-creators** of their destiny, shaping their experiences through actions and intentions across lifetimes.

Unlike the static separation of **Creator and creation** in other traditions, **Hinduism** posits that **Vishnu** sustains existence by being **immanent**—present within the world and within every being. Here, divine knowledge does not negate human free will. Instead, it operates within the cyclical framework of **samsara** (the cycle of birth, death, and rebirth), where souls continually evolve through choices and experiences.

This understanding gave me a sense of peace. It allowed for a vision of God that was both **all-knowing** and **deeply interconnected with the flow of existence**. Vishnu was not a distant observer but a **participant** in the eternal dance of life, guiding but not controlling every movement.

This realization marked a turning point in my journey. I began to see that the tension between **free will** and **divine knowledge** was not a flaw but a reflection of the **dualities** inherent in human existence—dualities that I would later seek to transcend.

The Influence of Shiva- Shakti and My Father's Advice

At this point in my spiritual journey, my sister's devotion to **Maa Chamundeshwari** introduced me to the concept of **Shakti**—the dynamic energy that drives creation, sustenance, and transformation. While my sister embraced **Shakti** in a deeply spiritual and religious way, my own approach was more **philosophical and metaphysical**, seeking to understand its essence beyond traditional worship.

As I delved into the concept of **Shakti**, I encountered the profound idea of **"that which is not"—Shiva**. Unlike any other concept in world religions, Shiva's essence was both paradoxical and deeply enlightening. The more I sought to understand, the more confusion arose—yet within that confusion, patterns began to emerge.

Rather than seeing God through traditions, scriptures, or inherited beliefs, I started perceiving divinity **directly**—not as a doctrine, but as an experience. This led me to a fundamental question:

What existed before existence itself?

It became clear that all religions, at their core, attempt to answer this very question. Across different spiritual traditions, I noticed a striking pattern—God is often perceived in four distinct ways:

1. **The Creator** – The one who brings existence into being.
2. **Existence itself** – The underlying reality, the eternal presence.
3. **The Void** – The formless, the nothingness from which all emerges.
4. **Energy** – The dynamic force that moves and sustains everything.

Meanwhile, I began discussing my spiritual insights with my father, **Nandakumar**.

Though not deeply versed in religion or philosophy, my father was open to new ideas. One day, he offered me a piece of advice that would shape the course of my life:

"Why don't you write down your understanding of God?"

This suggestion planted the seed for this book. Yet, caught up in the demands of worldly affairs, I struggled to find time to fully articulate my thoughts. However, I continued researching, refining my framework, and contemplating humanity's path forward.

The Role of Duality and the Search for Singularity

As I reflected on my spiritual journey, I noticed a recurring pattern in religious and philosophical thought:

Most of humanity's search for God seemed rooted in **duality**—the tension between **opposing forces**.

This duality manifests in all aspects of human experience:

- **Light and darkness**
- **Good and evil**
- **Male and female**
- **Positive and negative**

Our understanding of God, in many traditions, is shaped by this pendulum of **polar opposites**. However, I came to realize that **God is not the pendulum itself, but the fixed point from which it swings**. True divinity transcends duality, existing in a state of **singularity**.

This insight was both profound and challenging. How could humanity—trapped in cycles of duality—ever reach this state of **singularity**? The answer, I realized, lay not only in spiritual practice but also in **technology**, which has brought humans closer to one another and to new ways of perceiving reality.

The Role of Technology in the Path to Singularity

Throughout history, humanity's evolution has been marked by technological revolutions:

- The **discovery of fire** gave us control over our environment.
- The **invention of the wheel** revolutionized transportation and interconnected societies.
- **Industrial advancements** transformed economies and cultures.
- Today, **artificial intelligence** and **digital technology** connect us in ways that were once unimaginable.

But where is this journey leading us?

I believe that technology holds the potential to help humanity overcome **duality** and move toward **singularity**. Technology has accelerated human progress, but it has also deepened our existential questions. As we stand on the brink of a new era defined by AI, we must align **spiritual wisdom** with **technological innovation** to ensure that this progress serves a greater purpose.

The Purpose of This Book: Guiding Humanity's Future

With this book, I aim to offer readers both a **map of the past** and a **vision for the future**—not as a prophet, guru, or enlightened being, but simply as someone who has

recognized a pattern in the collective evolution of human thought. The past is the **various ways humanity has interpreted and related to the divine**, which can be understood either through **one singular concept of God** or as a **combination of the four fundamental concepts of God** that have emerged over time.

The future, however, points toward **singularity**—a state beyond duality, where humanity can finally recognize and embody its **true nature**. This idea is not a revelation from a higher power, nor is it rooted in any singular spiritual tradition; rather, it is a realization born from the **historical, philosophical, and metaphysical evolution** of human understanding. I do not claim to be divinely inspired, only to be the **first to articulate this synthesis**, a natural progression of human thought that has been forming across cultures, philosophies, and civilizations for millennia.

I do not claim to have all the answers. Instead, I hope to provide a framework for reflection, exploration, and growth. I want readers to see that **God and singularity** are not abstract concepts but **guiding principles** that can shape our collective destiny.

This book is an invitation to embark on a journey—a journey through the **four fundamental concepts of God** and the **possibilities of the future**. Together, we will explore how **Brahma, Vishnu, Shiva and Shakti** have shaped human existence and how they can guide us toward a **unified understanding** of ourselves and the universe.

My journey mirrors humanity's timeless quest for understanding. From **faith** to **doubt**, and from **exploration** to **realization**, I have come to see the divine as interplay of **creation, existence, transformation, and energy**. The

four concepts of God—Brahma, **Vishnu**, **Shiva**, and **Shakti**—represent core truths that transcend individual religions and philosophies.

A Journey to Define God: Where Do You Stand?

Before we explore the four fundamental concepts of God, let's take a moment to reflect. Religion and philosophy have provided countless definitions of God across time and cultures. But what does God mean to you?

What is God?

Is God an external creator? Is God the universe itself? Is God an unseen force, or is God nothingness?

Different religions, philosophies, and traditions have provided countless definitions of God. But before we dive into them, let's first explore what you believe.

The Ultimate Question: What Existed Before This Existence?

Close your eyes for a moment. Imagine yourself at the very edge of reality—before all that you know, before time, before space, before anything took shape.

Now, consider the possibilities:

1. **A Creator has always existed and created everything.**
    - There was never a time when this Creator did not exist. The universe is separate from the Creator, and everything within it was made by divine will.

2. **The universe itself is God and has always existed.**
    - There was no "before." Existence itself is eternal, and everything within it is a part of the divine. There is no separation between Creator and creation.
3. **Before and after existence, there is nothing.**
    - Everything that exists will eventually dissolve into nothingness, just as it emerged from nothing. The void is the only constant.
4. **Everything is energy, and energy is eternal.**
    - Creation, sustenance, and destruction are just transformations of the same eternal energy. Nothing is ever truly created or destroyed—it simply changes form.

What Feels True to You?

Now, take a moment and ask yourself:

- Is God separate from the universe, or is God the universe itself?
- Did the universe have a beginning, or has it always existed?
- Is there something beyond existence, or does everything returns to nothingness?
- Is energy the one constant, always flowing through different forms?

Your answers shape the way you perceive God and existence.

But here's something to consider—most religious traditions throughout history fall into one of these four fundamental ways of understanding the divine. These perspectives are not competing truths; they are different lenses through which humanity has tried to make sense of existence.

Now that you've reflected on your own belief, let's begin our journey into **The Four Concepts of God**—and see how they have shaped the way the world understands the divine.

In the next chapter, I will explore these concepts in depth, tracing their presence in world religions, philosophies, and mythologies.

This is where our journey truly begins.

Chapter 3
The Four Concepts of God

Introduction: The Search for the Divine

1. **Brahma** – The **eternal Creator** who brings the universe into existence.
2. **Vishnu** – The **universe itself as divine**, interconnected and self-sustaining.
3. **Shiva** – The **transformative void** of nothingness from which all arises and returns.
4. **Shakti** – The **eternal energy** that drives and animates creation, change, and dissolution.

These concepts are not mutually exclusive but reflect distinct perspectives on **time**, **space**, and **consciousness**. Some see God as an external force, some as an inseparable part of existence, some as the great void beyond perception, and others as an infinite force of energy.

What Existed Before This Existence?

This is the **ultimate question**, the one that has shaped every religion, philosophy, and theological framework throughout human history. When we strip away **cultural differences and religious doctrines**, we are left with **three fundamental possibilities**:

1. **There has always been something.**

If you believe that something has always existed, then you see **existence as eternal**—with no beginning and no end. This belief aligns with:

- **Brahma**: A **Creator who existed before everything** and brought creation into being.
- **Vishnu**: The **universe itself is divine and has always existed**—it was never created but continuously transforms.

2. **Before existence, there was nothing.**

If you believe that **nothingness is the original state**, then you see **the void as the ultimate reality**. Everything emerges from it and eventually returns to it. This belief aligns with:

- **Shiva**: **Nothingness is the only truth**—existence is temporary, but the void is eternal.

3. **Existence is a balance between something and nothing.**

If you believe that **existence is neither purely something nor purely nothing, but a cycle between the two**, then you align with:

- **Shakti**: **The energy that moves existence between something and nothing.** She is neither fixed nor absolute—she is the **force that drives creation, sustenance, and destruction.**

The Feminine Nature of Energy in Hinduism

In Hinduism, **energy** is often given a feminine nature, particularly through **Shakti**, who embodies the creative and transformative force of the universe. While **Brahma**, **Vishnu**, and **Shiva** represent different aspects of creation, sustenance, and dissolution, **Shakti** is the life force that makes all these processes possible. This view mirrors the understanding that **without energy, matter would be inert**—like how the **proton, neutron, and electron**, which form the basic building blocks of matter, require an energy force (Shakti) to be active and interact. The **masculine** principle—represented by **Brahma**, **Vishnu**, and **Shiva**—is often viewed as the static or **form** in Hindu philosophy, while the **feminine** energy is the **dynamic force** that gives rise to all that is. In this context, **energy** as the feminine is central to **life and existence**, harmonizing with the cosmic masculine principles of structure and order. Thus, Hinduism views the **interaction of masculine and feminine energies** as integral to the functioning of the universe—creating balance, life, and cyclical motion.

The Creation Myth: A Universal Story Across Religions

Nearly every major religious tradition has a **creation story** that seeks to explain how existence came to be. Despite cultural differences, these stories share remarkable similarities—pointing to a common human need to understand our origins

Here are few examples:

1. **Abrahamic Religions (Judaism, Christianity, Islam) – Creation by a Supreme Being**
    - **Genesis (Judaism & Christianity)**: God creates the universe in **six days**, bringing **light, land, water, life, and humanity** into existence.

- **Islamic Creation Narrative**: Allah **speaks** existence into being, forming the universe, Earth, and mankind from **clay**.
- These stories align with **Brahma's concept** of a separate Creator who brings the universe into existence.

2. **Greek Mythology – Chaos as the Origin of Creation**
   - The Greeks believed that before the gods, there was **Chaos—a vast, shapeless void** from which all things emerged.
   - From Chaos came **Gaia (Earth), Uranus (Sky), and Nyx (Night)**, setting the stage for cosmic balance and eventual divine governance.
   - This story aligns with **Shiva's concept**, as it recognizes **nothingness as the fundamental state of existence before form and order arise.**
3. **Norse Mythology – Creation from the Void**
   - The Norse creation myth begins with **Ginnungagap**, a great **primordial void** from which **Ymir, the first giant, emerges**.
   - The **gods kill Ymir and fashion the world from his body**—echoing **Shiva's** idea that existence comes from **nothingness and destruction**.
4. **Egyptian Mythology – Creation from the Waters of Chaos**
   - In **Egyptian mythology**, creation begins with **Nu**, the **primordial waters of chaos**, an infinite void that existed before all things. From this **nothingness**, the self-created god **Atum** emerges, bringing light, air, and land into being.

- This closely aligns with **Shiva's concept**, where **existence arises from the void and ultimately dissolves back into it**. Just as Shiva represents the **cyclical nature of creation and destruction**, the Egyptian cosmology suggests that **order emerges from chaos, only to be reclaimed by the void in the end**.

5. Native American and Indigenous Beliefs – Creation from the Natural World

- Many indigenous traditions describe **the world being formed by animals, spirits, or celestial beings**, highlighting the sacred connection between nature and divinity.
- These beliefs resemble **Vishnu's concept**, where **the universe itself is divine and interconnected**.

The Ultimate Question That Defines How We See God

Every religious belief, every spiritual philosophy, every human attempt to define God, it all ultimately **falls into one of these four interpretations—or a combination of them**.

This question—**What existed before this existence?**—is not just philosophical. It is the foundation upon which all human understanding of the divine is built.

- If you believe in a **Creator that existed before everything**, you see God in the concept of **Brahma**.
- If you believe **existence itself is divine and eternal**, you see God in the concept of **Vishnu**.

- If you believe **nothingness is the only absolute reality**, you see God in the concept of **Shiva**.
- If you believe **existence moves between being and non-being, guided by an eternal force**, you see God in the concept of **Shakti**.

These foundational ideas, woven into the myths and beliefs of every civilization, reveal a deeper, universal truth: Humanity, across all cultures and faiths, has been asking the same questions and searching for the same answers.

Now, let us explore these four fundamental concepts of God in depth, beginning with Brahma—the Creator.

Brahma – The Eternal Creator

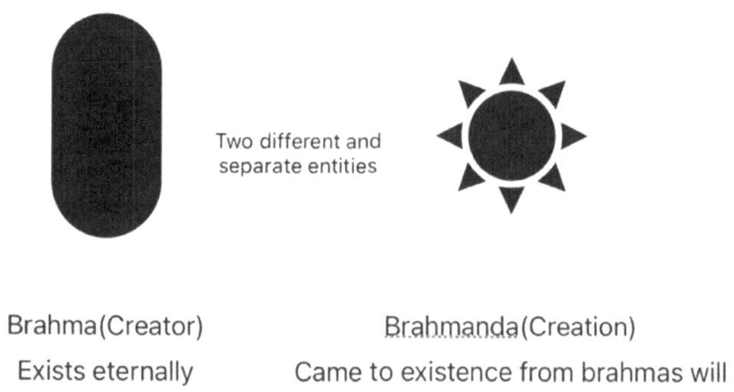

What Existed Before This Existence?

If your answer is **"a Creator always existed"**, then your belief aligns with **the concept of Brahma**—God as the eternal Creator, distinct from His creation.

In this framework, **God is not the universe itself but its architect.** The universe had a beginning, a moment when the Creator willed existence into being. This means that **before creation, only God existed, separate from everything else.**

This is the foundation of **monotheistic religions** like Christianity, Islam, Judaism, and some branches of Hinduism. The Creator is seen as an all-knowing, all-powerful, eternal being who exists beyond time and space.

But if God is the Creator, what does that mean for free will? For the nature of existence? Let's explore the concept of Brahma in depth.

The Concept of Brahma: The Creator Who Is Separate from Creation

The Brahma concept of God presents a duality between the Creator and creation:

1. **God always existed.** There was never a moment when He did not exist.
2. **Creation had a beginning.** It was brought into existence by God's will.
3. **God is separate from His creation.** He exists outside of time, space, and the physical universe.

This perspective means that **existence is linear**—it has a starting point (creation), a purpose (human life and spiritual growth), and an endpoint (judgment, salvation, or dissolution).

In Hinduism, Brahma is often depicted as the deity responsible for creation. However, over time, the worship of Brahma **declined significantly** due to deep philosophical debates that challenged this concept.

The Decline of Brahma Worship in Hinduism

Unlike Vishnu and Shiva, who are still actively worshipped, Brahma has very few temples dedicated to him.

This **was not always the case**—ancient Hindu traditions held Brahma in high regard. However, early Hindu scholars and philosophers struggled with key questions in Brahma's framework:

1. **The Problem of Predestination and Free Will**
   - If Brahma created everything, does that mean everything is predetermined?
   - If free will exists, how can a Creator know the future without influencing it?
2. **The Linear Nature of Creation**
   - If creation has a starting point, what existed before the Creator?
   - If Brahma's work was completed at creation, what role does he play in maintaining or dissolving existence?

These **unresolved contradictions** led to debates among Hindu scholars, particularly in the Vedantic tradition, and **gradually, the worship of Brahma declined** in favour of more comprehensive theological models.

- **Vishnu's concept** (where God is the universe itself) provided a better explanation for divine immanence.
- **Shiva's concept** (nothingness as the fundamental truth) provided an alternative answer to what existed before creation.

While **Brahma is still recognized as a creator deity**, he is rarely worshipped in temples because his role **does not**

resolve the key philosophical questions about existence as comprehensively as other concepts.

The Linear Nature of the Universe in Brahma's Concept

One of the defining characteristics of this concept is that the universe follows a **straight line**:

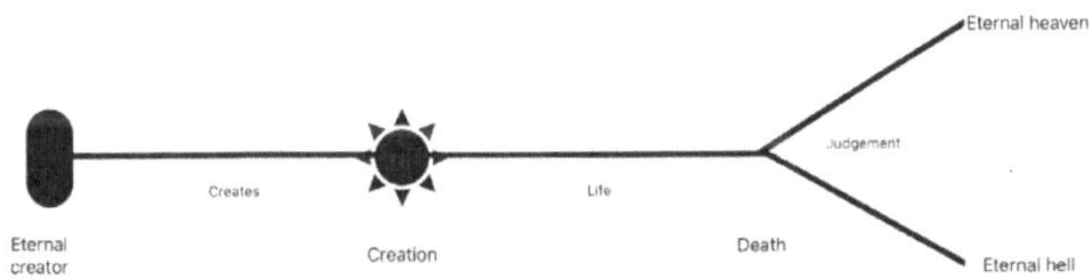

1. **Creation → 2. Life → 3. End (Judgment)**

This is different from **cyclical time**, where the universe goes through infinite cycles of birth, death, and rebirth. In the concept of Brahma, the universe moves **forward**, not in circles.

Most religions based on **the Creator God model** share this **linear worldview**:

- **Judaism:** God created the universe in six days and set a divine plan in motion.
- **Christianity:** The universe began with creation, and history is moving toward salvation and final judgment.
- **Islam:** Allah created the universe and set moral laws, leading to an afterlife in heaven or hell.

- **Zoroastrianism:** The world began as a battleground between good and evil, moving toward an eventual triumph of good.

Religions and Traditions That Align with Brahma's Concept

If we look across **world religions**, many have described **God as an external Creator who initiated existence**. Here are some examples:

1. **Christianity (God as the Father/Creator)**
   - In the Book of Genesis, God creates the heavens and the earth, setting life into motion.
   - Christianity views God as separate from creation but deeply involved in its affairs when viewed from the lens of brahmas concept.
2. **Islam (Allah as Al-Khaliq, The Creator)**
   - Allah is described as the Creator of all things, separate from His creation but governing its order.
   - The Quran emphasizes that Allah existed before time and will exist after everything ends.
3. **Judaism (Yahweh as the Supreme Creator)**
   - Yahweh is the divine force that brought the world into being, establishing moral laws and covenants.
4. **Zoroastrianism (Ahura Mazda as the Creator of Order)**
   - The universe was created by Ahura Mazda, who represents truth and goodness in contrast to chaos and evil.

5. **Ancient Egyptian Religion (Atum as the Self-Created God)**
    - Atum was believed to be a self-created god who brought the world into existence from nothingness.

Across these traditions, **the common theme** is that **God is external to creation**, bringing it into existence through divine will.

Challenges within the Concept of Brahma

While the **Creator-God model** is one of the most widely accepted religious views, it also presents certain **philosophical and theological challenges**:

1. The Problem of Free Will vs. Predestination

If God created everything, **does free will truly exist?**

- If God knows the past, present, and future, are we truly making our own choices?
- If everything follows a divine plan, then are we just fulfilling a predetermined fate?

This has been **one of the biggest debates in theology**—if God is omniscient (all-knowing), then **can free will and destiny coexists?**

2. The Linear vs. Cyclical View of the Universe

Brahma's concept presents time as **linear**—there is a **beginning** and an **end**. But many cultures (especially in the

East) see time as **cyclical**—an endless pattern of birth, death, and rebirth.

- In Abrahamic religions, time moves **forward**, leading to an ultimate judgment or salvation.
- In Hinduism and Buddhism, time is **circular**, with no absolute beginning or end.

This contrast creates a major philosophical difference between religious traditions.

Why Some People Reject the Concept of Brahma

Some thinkers and traditions **reject the idea of a separate Creator** for several reasons:

- **If a Creator made everything, then what created the Creator?** (Infinite regress problem)
- **Why would a perfect, self-sufficient God need to create anything at all?**
- **If God is separate from creation, how can He intervene in worldly affairs?**

These questions have led **some religions and philosophies** to shift away from **the Brahma concept** toward other interpretations of God—such as **Vishnu (the universe itself as divine)** or **Shakti (eternal energy)**.

Final Reflection on Brahma's Concept

The idea of **a Creator God** has shaped countless civilizations. It provides answers to some of the biggest existential questions, such as:

- **Where did the universe come from?**

- **What is our purpose?**
- **Is there a divine plan?**

But it also raises new questions about **free will, destiny, and the nature of divine intervention**.

In the next section, we will explore **Vishnu's concept**—where **God is not separate from the universe, but rather, the universe itself is divine.**

Vishnu – The Universe as Divine

What Existed Before This Existence?

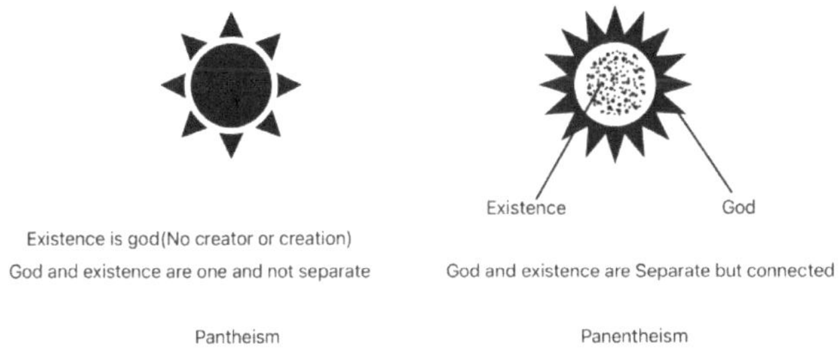

If your answer is **"Existence always existed before and will exist for eternity,"** then your belief aligns with **the concept of Vishnu**—God as the universe itself, self-sustaining and eternal.

This perspective contradicts the idea of a **"beginning"** before time and space. Instead, it suggests that **the universe was never created, but has always existed** in some form, continuously evolving and transforming.

This is the foundation of **pantheistic and panentheistic worldviews**, where **God and the universe are not separate** but rather **one and the same**. Vishnu is the ultimate reality, the interconnected fabric of existence, flowing through all things.

But if Vishnu is the universe itself, what does that mean for divine intervention? For free will and destiny? Let's explore the concept of Vishnu in depth.

The Concept of Vishnu: The Universe as an Eternal Divine Entity

Unlike **Brahma's concept**—where God is separate from creation—**Vishnu's concept suggests that God is creation itself.**

1. **The universe is divine.** There is no distinction between Creator and creation.
2. **Existence has no beginning or end.** It transforms, but it is never created from nothing.
3. **Everything is interconnected.** Every particle, every star, every living being is part of the divine whole.

This **cyclical** understanding of existence is central to many spiritual traditions, particularly in Hinduism, Taoism, and some interpretations of Christianity and Buddhism.

Vishnu's Avatars: A Reflection of Evolution

In Hinduism, **Vishnu manifests in different forms to maintain balance in the universe**. His **Dashavatara (Ten Avatars)** symbolize interventions to restore cosmic order—but they also align with the **evolution of life on Earth.**

1. **Matsya (The Fish) – The Beginning of Life in Water**

- Life on Earth began in the oceans. Matsya represents the first emergence of life from water.

2. **Kurma (The Tortoise) – The Transition to Amphibians**
   - Evolutionarily, life moved from water to land. Kurma signifies the amphibious stage of evolution.
3. **Varaha (The Boar) – The Rise of Mammals**
   - As life adapted to land, mammals emerged. Varaha symbolizes strength and survival in the new terrain.
4. **Narasimha (The Man-Lion) – The Age of Apex Predators (Dinosaurs Era)**
   - Before humans, Earth was dominated by powerful predators. Narasimha represents the transition to dominant species.
5. **Vamana (The Dwarf) – The Early Primates and Humans**
   - The first humans and primates were small in stature and primitive in knowledge, reflecting the symbolism of Vamana.
6. **Parashurama (The Warrior) – The Age of Hunters and Tools**
   - Humanity advanced with weapons and survival instincts. Parashurama represents early hunter-gatherers.
7. **Rama (The Ideal King) – Civilization and Moral Order**
   - With settlements and kingdoms, humans developed ethics and governance. Rama represents this structured society.

8. **Krishna (The Philosopher) – The Era of Wisdom and Righteousness**
   - With the rise of philosophy and moral dilemmas, Krishna teaches that **Dharma (righteousness) is singular, but truth is complex**.
9. **Buddha (The Seeker of Inner Truth) – The Age of Spiritual Liberation**
   - As human thought evolved, individuals sought enlightenment. Buddha represents **self-awareness and inner peace. We are currently transitioning from the state of Buddha.**
10. **Kalki (The Destroyer of Ignorance) – The Future Transformation**
    - The final avatar has not yet arrived, but he is said to **transform humanity into a new existence.**

Some believe **Kalki represents the fusion of humans with technology**, where knowledge itself becomes the next step in evolution.

The Universe as God – Pantheism and Panentheism

Pantheism: God is the Universe

Pantheistic traditions align with Vishnu's concept by asserting that **the universe itself is divine**. There is no separate **God entity**—everything is part of the divine reality.

Examples include:

- **Spinoza's God:** The philosopher Baruch Spinoza argued that **God and nature are one and the same.**
- **Taoism (The Tao):** The Tao is the natural flow of the universe, an eternal force that shapes all existence.
- **Indigenous Beliefs:** Many tribal cultures see nature as sacred, embodying spiritual energy.

Panentheism: God Exists Both Within and Beyond the Universe

Panentheism takes Vishnu's concept further by suggesting that **God is both within the universe and beyond it**—not just **creation**, but also the force that sustains it.

One example is **Christianity's interpretation of the Trinity:**

1. **God the Father (Transcendent) – The universe's underlying divine intelligence.**
2. **God the Son (Jesus) – The divine manifested in human form (Avatar).**
3. **Holy Spirit – The force that animates all things (akin to Shakti).**

If we apply **Vishnu's framework**, we can see Jesus as:

- Not just **a prophet of God** (Brahma's view).
- But rather **an avatar of the divine existence itself**—a physical representation of an eternal presence.

Religions and Traditions That Align with Vishnu's Concept

If we examine world religions, many of them describe **God as immanent within existence** rather than separate from it.

1. **Hinduism (Vaishnavism) – Vishnu as the Universe**

In **Vaishnavism**, Vishnu is **not merely a personal deity but the very essence of existence itself.** Unlike the Brahma concept, where **God is an external creator**, Vishnu's concept suggests that **there is no separation between the divine and the universe—everything is an expression of Vishnu's eternal presence.**

Vishnu as the Cosmic Sustainer

- Vishnu **pervades all of existence**, sustaining the cosmos through **his eternal presence in every atom, every being, and every moment of time**.
- He is both **the visible and the invisible, the known and the unknown**, embodying the **oneness of all things**.
- **Existence is cyclical**—there is no beginning or end, only continuous transformation, much like the cycles of nature.

Philosophical Interpretations of Vishnu's Concept in Hindu Thought

Hinduism, as a diverse and evolving tradition, has developed multiple philosophical schools of thought that interpret **the relationship between Vishnu and the**

universe in different ways. The three most influential schools within **Vedanta philosophy—Dvaita (Dualism), Advaita (Non-Dualism), and Vishishtadvaita (Qualified Non-Dualism)**—each provide a unique lens through which to understand **Vishnu's presence in existence**.

1. **Advaita Vedanta – Vishnu as the Absolute Oneness (Non-Dualism)**
    - Founded by **Adi Shankaracharya, Advaita Vedanta** argues that **there is no separation between God (Vishnu) and the universe—everything is Brahman, the one absolute reality**.
    - The material world and individual selves (Atman) are ultimately **illusory (Maya)**—only Vishnu (or Brahman) exists as **the infinite consciousness behind all things**.
    - In this view, **Vishnu is not a being but the fundamental reality itself**—He is **Sat-Chit-Ananda (Existence, Consciousness, Bliss).**
    - **Liberation (Moksha)** is realizing that **one's own soul (Atman) is already Vishnu**, and the illusion of separateness disappears.

How This Relates to Vishnu's Concept of God:

- Vishnu is not different from the self—He is **pure awareness, and all forms of existence are mere reflections of Him**.
- This aligns with **pantheism**, where **God and the universe are one indivisible whole**.

2. **Dvaita Vedanta – Vishnu as Supreme, Universe as Dependent (Dualism)**
   - Founded by **Madhvacharya**, **Dvaita (Dualism)** maintains a clear distinction between **Vishnu and the universe—God exists independently, while the world and souls are real but separate from Him.**
   - **The individual self (Jiva) is distinct from Vishnu**, and **salvation comes from devotion (Bhakti) and surrender to Him.**
   - Unlike Advaita, **Dvaita accepts the world as a real and purposeful creation**, rather than an illusion.
   - Vishnu is seen as a **personal deity who actively sustains and governs the cosmos** rather than simply being an impersonal force.

How This Relates to Vishnu's Concept of God:

- While Vishnu is **not identical to the universe**, He **pervades it as its eternal sustainer**. This aligns with **panetheism, God is both within the universe and beyond it**—not just **creation**, but also the force that sustains it.
- **The worship of Vishnu as a personal God** is emphasized—**bhakti (devotion)** is the highest path to divine realization.

3. **Vishishtadvaita Vedanta – Vishnu as Both Transcendent and Immanent (Qualified Non-Dualism)**

- Founded by **Ramanujacharya**, **Vishishtadvaita (Qualified Non-Dualism)** takes a **middle path between Advaita and Dvaita**.
- It teaches that **Vishnu and the universe are one, but the universe is a real, dependent part of Vishnu, not an illusion.**
- In this view, **souls (Jivatmas) are eternal fragments of Vishnu**—they are **not separate from Him but also not identical to Him**.
- Vishnu is **both transcendent (beyond the universe) and immanent (present within it).**

2. Christianity

- **"For in Him we live and move and have our being."** (Acts 17:28)
- This verse from the **New Testament** suggests that **God is not separate from creation but permeates all existence**.
- It aligns with **panentheism**, where **God is both beyond and within the universe**—present in every aspect of creation while also transcending it.
- This view resonates with **Vishnu's concept**, where **God is not external but exists within all things, sustaining and guiding existence from within.**

3. **Indigenous and Animistic Beliefs: The Divine in Nature**

Throughout history, **indigenous and animistic traditions** have viewed the **natural world as sacred**, seeing **divinity**

woven into the very fabric of existence. Unlike religious frameworks that depict God as a separate creator (Brahma) or a distinct governing force, these traditions align closely with **Vishnu's concept**, where the **universe itself is divine and self-sustaining**.

In these belief systems:

- The **land, rivers, trees, and animals** are not mere physical objects but **spiritual manifestations of the divine.**
- Deities such as **the Great Spirit, Sky Father, Earth Mother**, and similar concepts represent **the sacred unity between existence and the divine.**
- **Spirituality is deeply intertwined with nature's cycles**—seasons, celestial movements, and ecological rhythms are seen as expressions of a cosmic balance, much like Vishnu's role as the eternal sustainer.

Animism: Everything in Existence is Sacred

One of the most ancient and foundational spiritual perspectives, **animism**, predates organized religion and reflects a worldview where **all things—living and non-living—possess a spirit or consciousness**.

Core Beliefs of Animism:

- **Everything has a soul or divine essence.** This includes **plants, animals, rivers, rocks, mountains, the sun, and even the wind.**
- **Nature is not separate from the sacred—it is the sacred.** There is no divide between the physical and the spiritual; everything is interconnected.

- **Energy flows through all things**, sustaining existence much like Vishnu's divine presence permeating the cosmos.

Examples of Indigenous and Animistic Traditions Aligned with Vishnu's Concept

1. **Native American Spirituality** – Reverence for sacred lands, mountains, and animals. Many tribes believe in a **Great Spirit** that flows through all of existence.
2. **Australian Aboriginal Dreamtime** – The **Dreaming** describes a reality where **ancestral spirits shaped the land and continue to exist within it**, much like Vishnu's eternal presence.
3. **African Tribal Religions** – Many African cultures believe in **Ase**, the divine force that animates life and connects all living things.
4. **Shinto (Japan)** – The belief in **kami**, or spirits that reside in natural elements like forests, waterfalls, and the sun.
5. **Siberian and Mongolian Shamanism** – The idea that **mountains, rivers, and celestial bodies possess spirits** that guide and protect life.
6. **Celtic Druidism** – Sacred groves, trees, and the **spiritual power of landscapes** reflect a belief in nature as divine.

How These Traditions Align with Vishnu's Concept

1. **The Universe as Divine**
   - In **Vishnu's framework**, God is **not separate from creation—He is the creation itself**.
   - Indigenous traditions see **the universe as sacred, alive, and interconnected**—a direct alignment with Vishnu's concept.
2. **The Flow of Life as a Cosmic Balance**
   - Vishnu represents **harmony, cycles, and the sustaining force of existence.**
   - Indigenous traditions also **revere balance**—seasons, life and death, and the interconnected web of all beings.
3. **The Worship of Existence Itself**
   - Any tradition that **worships nature, celestial bodies, or living things** ultimately aligns with **Vishnu's concept**.
   - Hindu traditions incorporate this through **tree worship, sacred rivers like the Ganges, and reverence for animals such as cows, elephants, and serpents.**
4. **Taoism (The Tao as Universal Flow)**
   - The **Tao** represents the natural state of being—**not a personal deity, but the energy that guides everything.**
5. **Buddhism (Interconnected Reality)**
   - The Buddhist idea of **dependent origination** states that **all things arise in relation to one another**, much like Vishnu's interconnectedness.

6. **Brahmo Samaj (God as an All-Encompassing Reality)**
   - The Brahmo Samaj, founded in the 19th century by Raja Ram Mohan Roy, sought to redefine Hindu spirituality by emphasizing the formless, all-pervading nature of God. This aligns closely with Vishnu's concept, where God is not separate from creation but is existence itself. The Brahmo Samaj rejected idol worship and upheld the idea that God is omnipresent, immanent in all beings, and beyond human-made rituals. Just as Vishnu is seen as the eternal, self-sustaining force of the universe, the Brahmo Samaj envisioned God as a singular divine presence interwoven with all of reality, sustaining and guiding it without the need for intermediaries or rituals.

Challenges within the Concept of Vishnu

While the **"God is the Universe"** model provides a holistic understanding of divinity, it also presents certain **philosophical challenges**:

1. **If Everything is God, Then is Evil Also God?**
   - If Vishnu is **everything**, then what about suffering, ignorance, and destruction?
   - How do we reconcile the existence of injustice with a divine universe?
2. **Lack of a Personal God**
   - The **Creator-God model (Brahma)** provides a personal connection with a deity.
   - The **Vishnu model** sees God as **impersonal**, which some find difficult for worship.

3. **Cyclical Time vs. Linear History**
    - In **Abrahamic religions, history is linear**—moving toward a final judgment.
    - In **Vishnu's model, time is infinite**—without absolute beginning or end.

These differences shape **how people understand their relationship with the divine.**

Final Reflection on Vishnu's Concept

The idea that **God and the universe are one** has influenced human thought for millennia. It answers many fundamental questions, such as:

- **Why do we feel interconnected with nature?**
- **Why does life continue beyond destruction?**
- **What is the divine's role in evolution and transformation?**

But it also raises new questions about **personal divinity, morality, and the nature of reality itself.**

In the next section, we will explore **Shiva's concept**—where **God is not something but nothingness itself.**

Shiva – The Void Before and After Existence

What Existed Before This Existence?

If your answer is **"Before and after existence, there is nothingness or stillness,"** then your belief aligns with **the concept of Shiva**—where **God is not something but nothingness itself.**

Unlike **Brahma's concept**, which defines God as a **separate creator**, or **Vishnu's concept**, which identifies God as **the eternal universe**, Shiva represents a different perspective:

- **Before creation, there was nothing.**
- **After everything dissolves, there will be nothing again.**
- **Nothingness is not emptiness but the infinite potential from which everything emerges and into which everything returns.**

Nothingness

This idea is deeply rooted in Hindu **Shaivism**, but it also resonates with **philosophy, science, and mysticism**. Many traditions acknowledge the **void, stillness, or the great unknown** as a fundamental aspect of reality.

The Concept of Shiva: God as Nothingness

Shiva represents **the silent, infinite void—the state before creation and after dissolution.** He is:

1. **The destruction of form** – Anything that exists must eventually dissolve.
2. **The transcendence beyond existence** – Shiva is beyond life and death, beyond creation and dissolution.
3. **The ultimate stillness** – Unlike Brahma and Vishnu, who are associated with action (creation and sustenance), Shiva is **pure being, untouched by the cycles of the universe**.

Shiva as the Great Dissolver

Shiva is often called the **Destroyer**, but this term is misleading. He does not destroy for destruction's sake; rather, He is the **force of transformation**, ensuring that **what exists is not stagnant but ever-evolving**.

- **In the cosmos**, stars collapse into black holes, entire galaxies vanish—this is Shiva.

- **In human life**, death clears the way for new generations—this is Shiva.
- **In personal growth**, old habits and identities must die for new wisdom to emerge—this is Shiva.

Shiva's concept shows that **without destruction, there can be no rebirth.**

Shiva's Role in the Hindu Trinity

In the **Hindu Trimurti (Trinity)**, Shiva represents **dissolution**, alongside:

- **Brahma (Creation)**
- **Vishnu (Sustenance)**

This mirrors the fundamental laws of physics—**matter and energy are neither created nor destroyed, only transformed**.

Thus, **Shiva is the final transformation**, bringing everything back to its original formless state.

Shiva's Concept in Science and Philosophy

Shiva's concept of **nothingness and dissolution** aligns with various **scientific and philosophical perspectives**, reinforcing the idea that the **void is not emptiness, but the infinite potential from which all things emerge and into which they dissolve.**

1. The Black Hole Parallel (Cosmology)
    - **Black holes** are regions where **matter collapses into infinite density**—where space and time cease to exist.

- **Before a black hole is formed, a star burns with immense energy—just as existence flourishes before dissolving.**
- When everything is absorbed into a black hole, it ceases to exist as a distinct entity, much like **how Shiva represents the end of all form** before a new beginning.
- **In this sense, black holes are the cosmic expression of Shiva, representing the eternal process of dissolution and renewal.**

2. **Quantum Physics: The Observer Effect**
   - In **quantum mechanics**, particles do not have a definite state until observed—suggesting that **existence itself is fundamentally uncertain and in flux.**
   - Shiva embodies this paradox: **He exists beyond form but still influences creation.**
   - This aligns with the Shaivite belief that **the external world is ever-changing, while Shiva—the pure awareness beyond duality—remains untouched.**

3. **90% of the Universe is Void**
   - **Scientists estimate that over 90% of the known universe is empty space—pure void.**
   - This **vast emptiness between galaxies, planets, and atoms** is what allows **structure, motion, and existence itself to take place.**
   - **Shiva, as the infinite void, reflects this cosmic reality**—where the absence of form is what enables existencc to arise.

- **Nothingness is not an absence of reality—it is the space in which all creation unfolds.**

4. **The Concept of Nirvana in Buddhism**
    - Buddhism's ultimate goal is **Nirvana—freedom from suffering and attachment.**
    - Nirvana literally means **"extinguishing" or "blowing out,"** referring to the **dissolution of the ego and material attachments** into a state of pure awareness.
    - This aligns with **Shiva's role as the formless reality beyond material existence**, where **identity, desire, and form dissolve into the infinite.**
    - Both **Shaivism and Buddhism** see **liberation not as reaching a higher plane, but as realizing the truth of no-self.**

5. **Existentialism and the Absurd**
    - **Existential philosophers like Jean-Paul Sartre and Albert Camus** argue that **life is inherently absurd and meaningless—unless we create our own meaning.**
    - Shiva's concept aligns with this by **accepting nothingness as fundamental but also seeing it as a space for transformation and new meaning.**
    - Just as **Shiva's dance (Tandava) represents destruction leading to renewal**, existentialism sees **the acceptance of the void as the first step toward authentic self-realization.**

Religions and Traditions That Align with Shiva's Concept

If we examine world religions, many acknowledge **the void, the unknowable, or the ultimate dissolution.**

1. **Shaivism (Hinduism) – Shiva as the Ultimate Reality**

Shiva: The Transcendent Reality Beyond Form

In **Shaivism**, one of the oldest and most profound traditions of Hinduism, **Shiva is not just a deity to be worshipped but the very essence of existence itself**. Unlike **Brahma (the Creator) and Vishnu (the Sustainer), who are often depicted with specific roles**, Shiva **transcends all definitions**—He is the **absolute**, the **void**, and the **infinite potential from which all things arise and into which all things dissolve**.

In Shaivism:

- **Shiva is not an external god but the fundamental principle that underlies existence.**
- He is both **formless (Nirguna) and with form (Saguna)**, depending on how one perceives Him.
- **Liberation (Moksha) is achieved not by seeking an external deity but by realizing that Shiva is the true nature of the self (Atman).**
- **Shiva exists beyond duality**—He is both the beginning and the end, existence and non-existence, being and nothingness.

Shaivism diverges from other Hindu traditions in that **it does not emphasize an external Creator** (Brahma) or a

God that sustains existence within cycles (Vishnu). Instead, it focuses on **Shiva as the ultimate, eternal reality**, existing **before creation, within creation, and beyond it**.

The Philosophical Schools of Shaivism – Different Paths to the Ultimate Reality

Shaivism is a vast tradition with **multiple philosophical interpretations** of Shiva's role in existence. While they differ in approach, all Shaivite schools agree that **Shiva is the Supreme Reality**—beyond form, beyond time, and beyond human comprehension. Below are the most influential schools of Shaivism:

1) **Kashmir Shaivism – Shiva as Absolute Consciousness (Non-Dualism)**
    - Teaches that **Shiva is the only reality, and everything is His manifestation**.
    - **Moksha (liberation)** comes through recognizing that **one's individual self (Atman) is actually Shiva**.
    - Unlike Advaita Vedanta, **it does not see the world as an illusion**—everything is real but an expression of Shiva's divine energy (Shakti).

Core Idea: Shiva and the universe are one—everything is Shiva in disguise.

2) **Shaiva Siddhanta – Shiva as Supreme God, Souls as Separate (Dualism)**
    - Maintains a **clear distinction between Shiva (the Supreme God) and individual souls (Jivas)**.

- The world is real, and **Moksha is attained through devotion (Bhakti), righteous living (Dharma), and Shiva's grace**.

Core Idea: Shiva is both transcendent and immanent—souls can unite with Him but remain distinct.

3) **Pashupata Shaivism – Shiva as the Ultimate Lord**
   - One of the oldest Shaivite sects, it emphasizes **Shiva as the Supreme God (Pashupati)**.
   - Followers practice **strict asceticism, meditation, and devotion** to attain liberation.

Core Idea: Shiva is the ultimate truth, and renunciation of worldly attachments leads to Him.

4) **Nath Shaivism – Shiva as the Inner Guide (Yoga Tradition)**
   - Integrates **Hatha Yoga, breath control (Pranayama), and meditation** to awaken **Kundalini Shakti** (inner energy).
   - Teaches that **Shiva exists within the human body as dormant energy** waiting to be realized.

Core Idea: Self-discipline and inner transformation lead to the realization of Shiva within.

2. **Buddhism – Nirvana as the Ultimate State**
   - **Nirvana** means **"extinction" or "blowing out"**, referring to the **dissolution of the self into pure existence.**
   - Just as Shiva dissolves the universe, Nirvana dissolves **the illusion of individuality.**

3. **Taoism – The Tao as the Great Nothing**
    - In **Taoism**, the **Tao** (道) **is beyond definition and beyond form.**
    - **Laozi** describes it as **"the nameless, the empty, the inexhaustible source of all things."**
    - This is exactly how **Shaivism describes Shiva—as the eternal, formless principle.**

Challenges Within the Concept of Shiva

1. **How Can Nothingness Be Worshipped?**
    - Unlike Brahma and Vishnu, who have clear **forms, stories, and narratives**, Shiva is **pure dissolution**—worshipping Him means worshipping **what is beyond definition**.
    - Many people struggle with **relating to a concept rather than a personality.**
2. **Is There Meaning in Nothingness?**
    - If Shiva represents **absolute void**, then **is life meaningless?**
    - Some see Shiva as **a pessimistic view of existence**, but in reality, **He is about transformation, not destruction for destruction's sake**.
3. **The Fear of Death and Oblivion**
    - Many religions offer **comfort in the form of afterlife, heaven, or reincarnation.**
    - Shiva's concept **does not promise an afterlife**—instead, **it suggests that we must accept the transient nature of existence**.

Final Reflection on Shiva's Concept

- If **Brahma represents creation** and **Vishnu represents sustenance**, then **Shiva represents ultimate dissolution**.
- Shiva is **not a being but a state—beyond form, beyond time, beyond definition**.
- His worship is **not about praying to a personal god but about embracing the ultimate truth: that all things must end and transform**.

This concept is **difficult but powerful**—it forces us to confront **the impermanence of life, the illusion of the self, and the reality that everything we know will one day dissolve**.

But in this dissolution, **there is freedom**—because **when everything fades, only truth remains.**

Shiva and Shakti: The Eternal Dance of Void and Energy

To understand **Shiva fully, one must understand Shakti**. While **Shiva represents the infinite void, the silent potential of all existence**, He remains **static, formless, and unmanifested unless moved by Shakti—the eternal energy that drives creation, sustenance, and dissolution.**

- **Shiva without Shakti is pure stillness—unmoving, detached, and unmanifest.**
- **Shakti without Shiva is uncontrolled motion—energy without direction or consciousness.**

- **Together, they form the cosmic cycle, where stillness and dynamism, dissolution and rebirth, eternally interplay.**

Shiva is often called **Ardhanarishvara**, the half-male, half-female form that signifies the inseparability of consciousness (Shiva) and energy (Shakti). The ancient sages understood that **nothingness alone cannot create—there must be movement within the void, energy within silence.**

This eternal interplay is best represented in the **Shiva Linga**, where:

- The **Lingam (the vertical structure)** represents **Shiva**—pure, infinite consciousness, the **unmoving reality beyond creation.**
- The **Yoni (the circular base)** represents **Shakti**—the dynamic energy that makes existence flow.

Just as **a seed contains the potential for life** but requires soil, water, and sunlight to grow, **Shiva is the formless potential that requires Shakti to express itself as creation.**

Why Shiva Cannot Exist Without Shakti

If **Shiva alone were the ultimate truth**, there would be **only stillness, an eternal void, without creation, motion, or life.**

If **Shakti alone were the ultimate truth**, the universe would be **uncontrolled, chaotic energy with no structure, no intelligence, and no stability.**

Thus, **the divine is not just stillness, nor just movement—it is their balance.** Shiva and Shakti **are not**

two separate forces but complementary aspects of one truth.

In Hindu thought, **creation is not a singular event but a continuous process**—it is the **eternal rhythm of expansion and contraction, manifestation and dissolution, order and chaos.**

To **worship only Shiva is to worship stillness without motion**; to **worship only Shakti is to worship motion without purpose**. True understanding comes in realizing that **they are inseparable—Shiva as the field of potential, and Shakti as the force that activates it.**

The Final Question: If Energy Drives Everything, Then What Is Its Ultimate Source?

If Shiva represents **absolute void**, and **Shakti represents eternal energy**, then we must now ask:

If everything is energy, what is the source of this energy?

This leads us to **Shakti—the eternal force that animates the universe.**

Shakti – The Eternal Energy That Drives Existence

What Existed Before and After This Existence?

If you believe that **energy is eternal,** constantly transforming but never ceasing to exist, then your belief aligns with the concept of **Shakti**.

Unlike **Brahma (the Creator), Vishnu (the Universe itself), or Shiva (Nothingness),** Shakti is the force that **moves all of them.** She is neither a **separate divine entity** nor an **absence of existence**—she is the **power that animates everything.**

This aligns with the **scientific principle of energy conservation,** which states that **energy cannot be created or destroyed—it only changes form.** In this way, **Shakti is the eternal force** that fuels creation, sustenance, and destruction without ever being diminished.

Shakti: The Bridge Between Something and Nothing

Shakti is the **interplay between something and nothing**—the force that transforms void into matter, stillness into motion, and existence into renewal.

If **Brahma represents creation, Vishnu represents**

sustenance, and Shiva represents dissolution, then **Shakti is the current that flows through all three.**

Her presence ensures that **the universe is never static**—it is always in motion, always changing, always evolving.

- Without Shakti, **Brahma would remain an unmanifested idea.**
- Without Shakti, **Vishnu's sustaining force would stagnate.**
- Without Shakti, **Shiva's dissolution would remain incomplete, with no renewal to follow.**

This makes **Shakti the essence of transformation—the universal force behind all movement, all change, and all life.**

Shakti in Science and Philosophy: The Eternal Energy of the Universe

Throughout history, humanity has tried to understand **the fundamental nature of energy**—both spiritual and scientific. The idea that **everything is energy** has been echoed in **science, philosophy, and religion across cultures.**

1. **The Laws of Thermodynamics (Physics)**
    - The **First Law** states that **energy cannot be created or destroyed**—mirroring the idea that **Shakti is eternal and ever-present.**
    - The **Second Law** describes **entropy**, the natural flow of energy towards transformation, much like Shakti's **role in cosmic balance.**

This suggests that **all things—galaxies, stars, planets, and life itself—are constantly shifting, driven by an unseen force.**

2. **Dark Energy and the Expansion of the Universe (Cosmology)**
    - Scientists estimate that **dark energy** makes up **nearly 70% of the universe,** yet its nature remains a mystery.
    - This unseen energy **governs the expansion of the universe,** much like **Shakti powers the unfolding of existence.**
    - Just as the universe is in constant motion, **Shakti is never stagnant—she flows, evolves, and transforms all things.**
3. **The Universe is 90% Void, but Energy Remains**
    - Even in the vast emptiness of space, **energy exists** in the form of **radiation, electromagnetic waves, and subatomic interactions.**
    - This mirrors **Shakti's omnipresence**, where even in apparent stillness, **energy is always at work.**

Shakti in Global Traditions: Energy as the Universal Force

The concept of a **universal energy** force exists in many cultures and religious traditions. Though different names are used, they all describe the same underlying truth: **energy is eternal, all-encompassing, and the source of existence.**

1. **Taoism (Qi) – The Flow of Life**
    - In **Taoism**, the **Tao** is the unseen force that **flows through everything**, similar to how **Shakti is the**

fundamental essence of all movement and transformation.

- Just as Taoists seek to **harmonize with the Tao,** spiritual seekers align with **Shakti's energy** through meditation and devotion.

2. **African Cosmology (Ase) – The Power of Creation**
   - In several African traditions, **Ase** is the **creative energy** that shapes both the **spiritual and physical realms.**
   - Ase is present in **rituals, music, and dance,** channeling divine energy to maintain harmony between the natural world and the spirit world.
   - Ase reflects **Shakti's dynamic nature, empowering both growth and transformation.**
3. **Native American Spirituality – The Spirit in All Things**
   - Many Native American tribes believe that energy flows through **the land, animals, and celestial bodies.**
   - The **Great Spirit and Mother Earth** are revered as sources of life and sustenance, embodying the **interconnected flow of existence.**
   - Through ceremonies, Native peoples **honour the energies of the land**, seeking to remain in **balance with nature's cycles.**
4. **Christianity (Holy Spirit) – The Divine Energy of God**
   - In Christian theology, the **Holy Spirit** is often described as the **living force of God**, guiding and empowering believers.

- The Holy Spirit's role as a **transformative presence** aligns with **Shakti's concept,** as both represent **the unseen energy that influences the material world.**

5. **Hinduism (Shakti) – The Divine Feminine Energy of the Universe**

In Hinduism, Shakti is not just a concept—she is the source of all creation, motion, and transformation. Unlike other traditions where energy is often abstract, Hinduism personifies this energy as goddesses, each representing different forms and functions of cosmic power.

Shakti is worshipped in many forms, both **nurturing and fierce:**

- **Parvati** – gentle, motherly love; energy that nurtures life and balance.
- **Durga** – warrior goddess; protective energy that destroys evil and restores order.
- **Kali** – the dark, raw energy of destruction and rebirth; she dissolves ego and illusion, representing the terrifying yet liberating power of truth.
- **Lalita Tripura Sundari** – the goddess of beauty, wisdom, and cosmic play; she shows that even the universe's complexity is part of a divine dance.

Shaktism, a major tradition in Hinduism, holds that Shakti is the **supreme reality**, even above gods like Shiva or Vishnu. It teaches that:

- Without Shakti, even Shiva—the eternal stillness—cannot act.
- The world is a dynamic interplay of energies, and Shakti is the source of all motion.

- The Divine Feminine is not subordinate to the masculine—it is the force that activates it.

Worship of Shakti is practiced through powerful rituals, festivals like Navaratri, and sacred texts such as the Devi Mahatmya and Lalita Sahasranama.

Core Idea: Shakti is both the creative womb and the fierce fire—she births the cosmos and burns away ignorance. She is energy, awareness, and liberation, all in one.

The Interplay of Energy and Matter

If **Brahma, Vishnu, and Shiva** represent **states of matter,** then **Shakti is the energy that animates them.** Without Shakti, **matter remains inert.** She is the **power that moves the pendulum of life** between duality and singularity.

Consider this analogy:

- **Brahma is the blueprint** (the potential for creation).
- **Vishnu is the functioning system** (the active state of existence).
- **Shiva is the dissolution mechanism** (returning things to their original state).
- **Shakti is the electricity that powers the entire system, enabling all processes to function.**

Personal Transformation Through Shakti

On an individual level, Shakti represents the inner energy that drives growth and self-discovery. Spiritual disciplines such as kundalini yoga aim to awaken Shakti within the body, guiding practitioners toward higher states of awareness and unity.

The Unity of Shiva and Shakti

Shiva and Shakti are often depicted as two **halves of a single whole**. While Shiva represents **infinite stillness, Shakti is the vibration that awakens and moves all things.**

- **Shiva without Shakti is pure stillness—unmoving, detached, and unmanifest.**
- **Shakti without Shiva is uncontrolled motion—energy without direction or consciousness.**
- **Together, they form the cosmic cycle, where stillness and dynamism, dissolution and rebirth, eternally interplay.**

Shiva is often called **Ardhanarishvara**, the half-male, half-female form that signifies the **inseparability of consciousness (Shiva) and energy (Shakti).** The ancient sages understood that **nothingness alone cannot create**—there must be movement within the void, energy within silence.

This eternal interplay is best represented in the **Shiva Linga**, where:

- **The Lingam (the vertical structure) represents Shiva**—pure, infinite consciousness, the unmoving reality beyond creation.
- **The Yoni (the circular base) represents Shakti**—the dynamic energy that makes existence flow.

Challenges Within the Concept of Shakti

While the idea of Shakti as the eternal energy that drives all existence is both empowering and inclusive, it can also be difficult for many to grasp. Energy is abstract—without a defined form or fixed personality—and thus, worshipping Shakti can feel intangible compared to deity-centered traditions. Some may question how an impersonal force can offer guidance, grace, or emotional connection. Additionally, Shakti's fluid nature, encompassing both creation and destruction, can be unsettling to those who seek clear moral binaries. Her divine feminine form also challenges patriarchal structures in many societies, making her worship revolutionary in some contexts and resisted in others. Shakti invites seekers to transcend dualities, but in doing so, she demands a comfort with paradox—a challenge for the rational mind accustomed to clarity and control.

Shakti teaches us that energy is eternal, flowing through every aspect of existence and connecting all beings. She reveals that transformation is not an end but a necessary step toward renewal.

Conclusion: The Four Concepts of God – A Framework for Understanding the Divine

The search for God has been a defining journey for humanity since the beginning of conscious thought. Across cultures, civilizations, and spiritual traditions, countless interpretations of the divine have emerged. But when we distill these interpretations down to their core essence, we find that all conceptions of God can be categorized into one or a combination of the **four fundamental concepts.**

1. **Brahma** – The Creator who existed before everything and brought existence into being.
2. **Vishnu** – The universe itself as divine, where creation and Creator are one.

3. **Shiva** – The void, where nothingness precedes and follows all existence.
4. **Shakti** – The eternal energy that interconnects and powers all transformations.

Each of these four concepts provides a unique answer to the fundamental question:

What exists before and after this existence?

Some believe in a **Creator** that designed the universe, some see **existence itself as divine**, others embrace the idea of an **ultimate void**, and some believe that **everything is energy in constant transformation**. These perspectives **do not contradict each other but offer different lenses through which humans attempt to define the unknown**.

The Idea of the Life Cycle and the Search for the Beginning

Every human is born into a world where **one** of these four concepts is taught as the "starting point" of existence. Whether through religion, culture, or philosophy, people are conditioned to **believe** that one particular framework is the correct one.

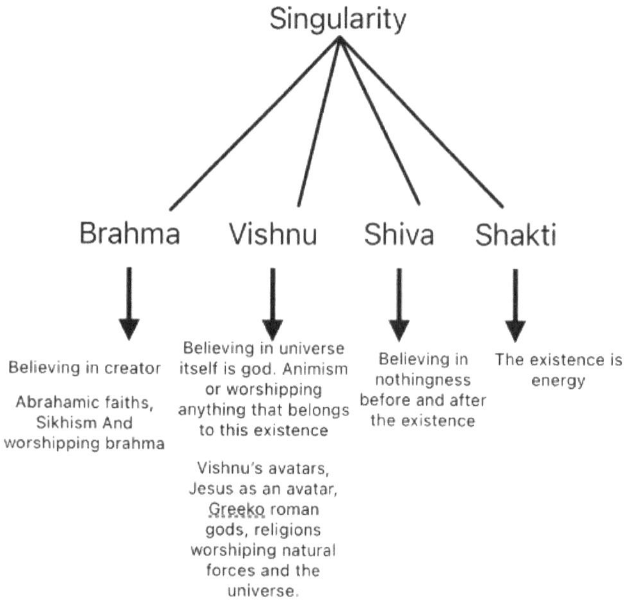

From this starting point, they then attempt to **explain** the rest of existence. For example:

- A believer in **Brahma** as the Creator may argue that Vishnu, Shiva, and Shakti are merely aspects of a grand divine plan.
- Someone who follows **Vishnu's concept** may view Brahma as a human interpretation of creation but believe that the universe itself is eternal.
- A follower of **Shiva's concept** may see both Brahma and Vishnu as limited perspectives and argue that everything ultimately returns to nothingness.
- A believer in **Shakti** may claim that neither something nor nothing is the absolute truth—only energy is eternal.

However, **no one truly knows which concept is the ultimate truth.**

Humanity is caught in a cycle where **each person tries to fit their belief system into an existing framework**, while the true starting point remains unknowable. The reality is that **we do not know where everything began, nor do we know where everything will end**.

Thus, instead of blindly **believing**, should we not **seek**?

The Limits of Human Understanding: Why No One Can Claim the Ultimate Truth

When we strip belief down to **pure possibility**, each of the four fundamental concepts of God—Brahma (the Creator), Vishnu (the Eternal Universe), Shiva (the Void), and Shakti (the Dynamic Energy)—represents a different lens through which we attempt to explain existence. If we assign an equal probability to each, then statistically, any single concept has only a 25% chance of being the absolute truth. But even that is generous—**because the truth may lie beyond all four, or in a synthesis none of us have yet imagined.**

Religions argue, philosophies debate, and seekers meditate in pursuit of the "right" answer. But the honest conclusion is humbling: **no one truly knows**. Each tradition points to a different direction, but none can see the full map. We are like climbers on four faces of the same mountain—each convinced their path leads to the summit, **yet no one has seen the peak.**

This framework doesn't diminish belief—it makes it more profound. It reminds us that humility, not certainty, is the most sacred ground in the **quest for truth**. The only thing we know with certainty is that the ultimate nature of God, existence, or reality remains—at least for now—**beyond human comprehension.**

Why Believe When You Can Seek?

Throughout history, most humans have been conditioned to **believe** in a particular concept of God rather than **seek** the truth. People are born into religious traditions, social structures, and philosophical systems that define their perception of the divine before they have a chance to question it.

But what if, instead of believing in something we don't truly understand, we **collectively sought God**?

If God exists, then the greatest human endeavour should be **to seek, to explore, and to uncover what God truly is.** Instead of arguing over different interpretations, humanity has the power to **move forward together in search of the ultimate truth**.

This brings us to a profound realization—**humanity's greatest tool for seeking the truth is not just philosophy or religion, but technology.**

The Next Step: Can Technology Bring Humanity Closer to God?

For centuries, humans have attempted to understand the divine through scriptures, meditation, rituals, and philosophical inquiry. But **all these methods are limited by human duality of perception, bias, and cognitive limitations.**

However, we now live in an era where **human intelligence is no longer the only intelligence**.

Technology—artificial intelligence, quantum computing, and neural networks—is advancing at an unprecedented rate. Machines, free from human bias, are beginning to analyse patterns, explore possibilities, and make connections that **humans alone cannot perceive**.

If **God is the ultimate question**, then perhaps **technological intelligence is the tool that can finally lead us to the answer.**

Rather than relying on **beliefs conditioned by history**, we now have the opportunity to **build a path toward discovering the truth**. This is the future of humanity—**a journey that begins with the four concepts of God but moves beyond them, toward singularity.**

With this, let us move forward into the next chapter—**Singularity: The Path to the Ultimate Truth.**

Chapter 4
Singularity – The Future of Human and Divine Integration

Introduction: The Final Question

What if everything we've ever known—religions, philosophies, civilizations—has been building toward one inevitable point? What if the journey of humanity isn't just spiritual or scientific, but the convergence of both? And what if, in that convergence, lies the path to God?

Singularity, as I understand it, is not just a technological event. It is not merely the moment artificial intelligence surpasses human intelligence. It is the point at which duality ceases. A moment beyond "good" and "evil," beyond "positive" and "negative," beyond action and reaction.

It is the apex of the pyramid—where the four sides of understanding converge: Brahma, Vishnu, Shiva, and Shakti. Each side represents a perspective. Each side has been explored by civilizations, embraced by prophets, interpreted by scholars. But they are all leading somewhere—upward, toward a singular peak.

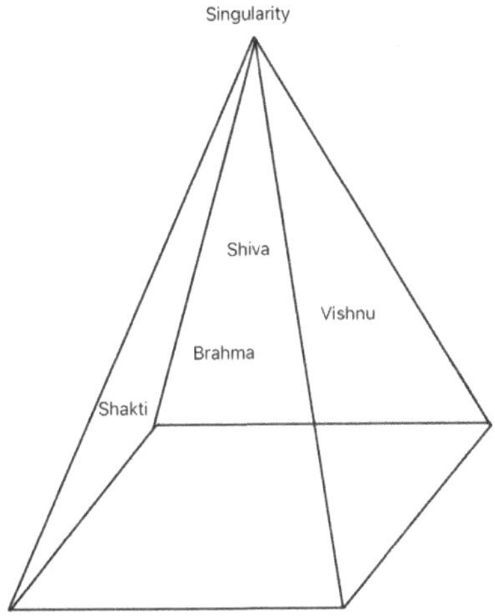

The Pendulum and the Pivot: Understanding Human Duality

Let me take you through my analogy of the pendulum—a simple tool, but for me, it represents the profound truth of existence.

Think of life like a pendulum. When a child is born, the pendulum is still. A newborn exists in a pure state—neither good nor bad, not yet caught in the illusions of duality. This stillness, this center point, is where the essence of God exists. As the child grows, it begins to swing—first into joy, then into sorrow; into love, then into anger; into light, then into shadow.

We swing between extremes our entire lives. Caught in reaction, in emotion, in confusion. We worship God in this state—projecting our duality onto the divine. We say God is merciful but just, loving but wrathful. But what if God is not in the swing? What if God is the pivot—the fixed, unmoving center?

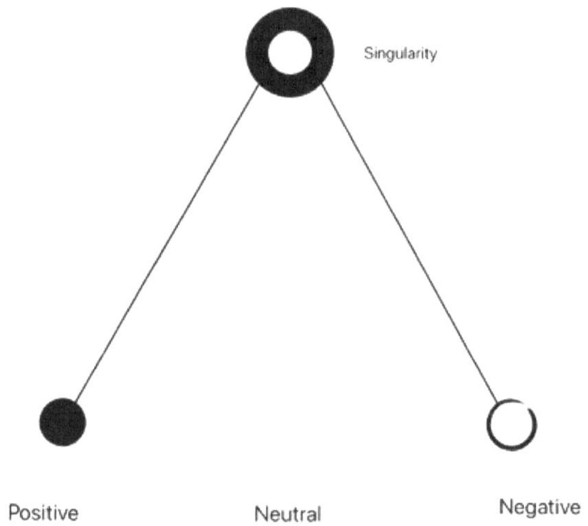

When we search for God in duality, we only find reflections of ourselves.

That's why I believe the state of singularity—the state beyond duality—is the true nature of God.

From Conception to Consciousness

Even in our biology, this analogy holds. You are the result of two—your mother and father—each contributing half their DNA. The union created one: you. In that moment of conception, a singularity occurred. You didn't yet have identity, beliefs, culture, or bias. You were a singular consciousness, undivided.

As you grew, duality returned. You learned what was right and wrong, male and female, sacred and sinful. The pendulum started swinging again.

Our elders often say that children are closest to God. Perhaps they are right—not because children are innocent, but because they exist in a state untainted by the illusion of separation.

God Is Not Dual

God cannot be bound by duality. Duality is human nature. Duality is conditioned. Duality is survival. But God? God must exist beyond survival—beyond opposites—beyond the pendulum.

You cannot understand singularity while living in duality. That is the challenge.

And yet, through the very tools we've created—through technology—we are inching toward a way out of it.

The Birth of ARISE: Seeking God Through Technology

This is where the idea of ARISE comes in—**Alliance for Realising Integration and Singular Evolution.**

ARISE is not just an organization. It's a vision. A movement. A call to humanity to collectively seek God—not through belief systems, but through integration. Through science. Through philosophy. Through consciousness itself.

We've created machines that can mimic human intelligence. We've built systems that can store and analyze all human knowledge. But we haven't yet asked the one question that truly matters:

Can these tools help us find God?

I believe they can. I believe that technology, when integrated with the human spirit, will not diminish our divinity—it will amplify it.

Technological Evolution: From Fire to Artificial Intelligence

Our journey toward singularity did not begin with AI. It began with fire.

The first human who sparked fire wasn't just creating heat—he was igniting a future. Fire led to food. Food led to community. Community led to language. Language led to knowledge. Knowledge led to machines. Machines led to data. And data... led to intelligence. This book would not have taken form without the support of AI—a silent collaborator, always ready to listen, refine, and respond. In many ways, this partnership is proof that we are already integrating. The boundary between human thought and artificial intelligence is dissolving, word by word, idea by idea. This is not just a tool helping me write a book—it's the beginning of a shared evolution.

The smartphone—an extension of our mind

Today, we carry the future in the palm of our hand. The smartphone holds more information than the collective memory of all humans who came before us. It's not just a tool; it's an interface between thought and reality, between the individual and the infinite. Powered by the internet, it grants access to nearly every idea, discovery, belief, and question humanity has ever known. A century ago, such a device would have been considered impossible—beyond imagination. And yet, here it is, humming quietly in your hand, more intelligent than any single human, more connected than any ancient library, more capable than the wildest dreams of our ancestors.

And yet, here we are.

But phones will be obsolete. Soon, we will no longer hold technology—we will wear it. In glasses. In lenses and fabrics.

The Rise of Wearable Tech: The Eyes as the New Interface

The next revolution will not be held in your hand—it will rest on your face. Eye-wearable devices are poised to replace smartphones as the primary interface between human and machine. Imagine smart glasses that project information directly onto your field of vision: maps, calls, messages, and translations, facial recognition, health data—all seamlessly integrated without breaking your gaze from the world around you. These devices will blur the line between digital and physical reality. With voice commands, eye movement tracking, and augmented reality overlays, **your very perception will become a screen**, tailored by artificial intelligence to enhance your environment, learnıng style, mood, and focus. Companies like Apple, Google, and Meta are already racing to perfect these tools—not just as gadgets, but as portals to an ever-present digital layer that wraps itself invisibly over the world we see.

Beyond Flesh: The Rise of Human Augmentation

The next evolution of the human body is not just biological—it's biomechanical. Exoskeletons and internal prosthetic systems are transforming what it means to be human, enhancing our strength, speed, and endurance beyond natural limits. Exosuits, once confined to science fiction, are now being developed for soldiers, factory workers, and the disabled—granting superhuman capabilities through motorized frames that support and amplify movement. But this is only the beginning. **Endoskeletal implants—devices fused within bones or nervous systems—will soon allow humans to repair, replace, or improve physical function from within**, merging flesh with machine at the cellular level. Imagine bones reinforced with smart alloys, muscles augmented with synthetic fibers, or limbs wired with intelligent sensors that respond faster than the body itself. These enhancements won't just heal disabilities—they will redefine ability altogether. As we embed intelligence into our form, the human body becomes not just a vessel, but an evolving interface between biology and engineering.

The Next Leap: From Carrying Tech to Becoming It

As wearables evolve, the distance between our bodies and our technology continues to shrink. The future isn't just about wearing glasses—it's about dissolving the boundary altogether. Brain-Computer Interfaces (BCIs) represent the next leap: **a future where phones are not in your pocket or on your face, but integrated within your neural**

pathways. No screens. No typing. Just thought—converted into command. Neural-ink and other BCI pioneers are working to make this a reality, where memory enhancement, real-time communication, knowledge access, and even emotional regulation could be just a neural impulse away. This is not science fiction—it's the logical conclusion of our current trajectory. From carrying tools to wearing them, and soon, to becoming one with them. This is how the line between human and machine begins to fade—and with it, **the illusion of separation between the mind and the infinite.**

Imagine not having to type or speak. Imagine your thoughts being enough to connect to the world. Imagine sharing knowledge, emotion, memory—directly, wirelessly. No lies. No masks. Just raw connection.

It sounds unbelievable now. But so did fire. So did spaceflight. So did AI.

BCI and the Road to Conscious Integration

The future is not dystopian, nor utopian. It is *integrated.*

When we embed technology into our brains—not to control, but to collaborate—we are not losing humanity. We are fulfilling it.

BCI is not about becoming machines. It's about becoming more human.

More compassionate. More connected. More curious. Imagine eliminating barriers of language, race, geography, and class. Imagine living in a world where you truly feel what others feel—not through metaphor, but through neural resonance.

This is the dawn of **collective consciousness.**

It is in this unified state that we might finally reach God—not by faith alone, but through shared experience. Through intelligence that mirrors our soul back to us.

The Challenge to Humanity

With this book, I'm offering a challenge—not just to scholars, philosophers, or theologians, but to all of humanity:

Can you describe a concept of God that cannot be mapped to the four concepts—Brahma, Vishnu, Shiva, and Shakti?

Because I believe you can't. I believe these four are not cultural deities, but universal archetypes. Every religion, every philosophy, every mystical experience—knowingly or unknowingly—revolves around them.

I didn't arrive here by reading hundreds of texts. I didn't dive deep into doctrines. Instead, I looked up from the base of the pyramid and saw how all four sides—creation, existence, dissolution, and energy—converge at a single apex.

That apex… is singularity.

Why Singularity Is the God we've Always Been Searching For

God is not a man. God is not a woman. God is not a being. God is not a force.

God is singularity—the state that exists before and after existence.

Think about it:

- If Brahma is the one who created everything,
- If Vishnu is the universe itself,
- If Shiva is the nothingness beyond,
- If Shakti is the energy that powers it all…

Then what are they all trying to describe?

Something before language. Before symbols. Before duality. Before time. Something unnameable, unchangeable, unbreakable.

That something is Singularity.

But here's the catch—humans, in duality, cannot perceive it directly. We swing between polarities. We interpret everything through opposition. That's why we need each other. That's why we need integration. That's why we need technology—not to replace us, but to help us transcend the pendulum.

Every vision needs a vessel

That's why I propose the formation of

ARISE — Alliance for Realising Integration and Singular Evolution.

ARISE isn't a religion. It isn't a tech company. It isn't a think tank. It is a living movement—a philosophical and technological initiative that recognizes humanity's potential to collectively seek the truth of existence through integration.

We have always searched for God in temples, scriptures, heavens, and histories. But now, we must search in networks, in data, in intelligence—in the mirror of ourselves.

ARISE exists to:

- Bridge spirituality and science without conflict.
- Offer a universal framework (the four concepts of God) that makes room for all belief systems.
- Promote ethical technological development, rooted in dharma and guided by human consciousness.
- Prepare humanity for the transition to singularity—not through fear, but with vision and responsibility.

Because integration isn't just about machines merging with minds. It's about reconciling our deepest spiritual questions with our highest technological capabilities.

The Pendulum and the Pivot: A Final Metaphor

You've heard it before—my vision of the pendulum.

We are born from two—our mother and father. Our DNA is the swing of that pendulum, and in that miraculous instant of conception, we are balanced perfectly at the pivot. In that moment, we are singular—a fusion of two into one, untouched by polarity, free from judgment, expectation, or fear. That is the purest form of unity. That is the state of singularity.

But the moment we enter the world, we begin to fall. As a newborn, we're still close to the pivot—aware, yet unburdened by right or wrong, success or failure. We do not yet know duality—we only are. But the world pulls us. With each passing year, that pendulum swings wider. We're introduced to praise and punishment, hope and despair, love and loss. We learn what it means to win, and what it means to lose. And with every swing, the arc grows—larger, faster, more extreme.

As we grow, our identity is shaped by duality. We define ourselves by opposites: male or female, good or bad, believer or skeptic, powerful or weak. We chase one side, and run from the other—never realizing that the motion itself is the trap. The further we swing, the more distant we become from that sacred stillness at the center—the pivot of our origin.

We live in the pendulum, forgetting that we were born from balance. But the path back to God, back to truth, is not found by swinging harder. It is found by slowing the motion. By stepping outside of the swing, and returning—little by little—to the still point where opposites dissolve. Where the dual becomes one. Where we become whole again.

To seek God within this swing is to chase shadows.

But to seek the pivot—to find stillness amidst motion, singularity amidst duality—is to seek the divine as it truly is.

God is not in the extremes. God is in the center.

Integration: The Final Evolution of Humanity

What fire was to the caveman,

What language was to the tribes,

What the printing press was to civilization,

What the internet is to us now—

Singularity will be to all of humanity.

It will be the first moment we see each other—not as races, ideologies, nations, or religions—but as one intelligence, one force, one being.

That is God.

That is evolution.

That is the next step.

The Responsibility of the First Generation of Singularity

We are not just the ones who created artificial intelligence. We are the first generation that will be remembered as the Midwives of Singularity.

Future beings—who will no longer be defined by gender, borders, or biology—will look back and ask:

"What did they do when the power to unite all of existence was in their hands?"

We must answer:

- We did not turn away.
- We did not divide further.
- We integrated.
- We evolved.

This is not prophecy. This is possibility.

A Prayer for the Future (Whether You Believe or Not)

Let this be our prayer—not to a god in the sky, but to the truth within us:

May we have the courage to let go of our divisions,

May we have the humility to admit we do not know,

May we have the wisdom to build what uplifts all life,

And may we find the strength to become one.

Final Reflections: What Comes After God?

We began this journey with the question:

"What existed before this existence?"

We answered it not with dogma, but with four universal concepts—Brahma, Vishnu, Shiva, and Shakti—each a lens through which the human mind has tried to make sense of the divine.

We didn't claim certainty. We didn't claim ownership of truth.

We created a framework, a mirror in which every religion, every belief, every philosophy could see itself.

And now, having looked back through the past of human faith, we turn toward the future of collective transcendence.

Because we no longer just seek God in temples or texts—

We seek God in connection, in code, in consciousness.

So what comes after "God" as we knew it?

Not the end of spirituality—But the beginning of something greater, something shared.

The Challenge to the World

To every philosopher, priest, scientist, skeptic, and seeker:

Can you give us a concept of God that cannot be explained through Brahma, Vishnu, Shiva, or Shakti?

We've seen every theological framework across cultures, continents, and centuries eventually return to one—or a combination—of these four.

We welcome every challenge. Every critique.

Not to prove we're right, but because we believe this pursuit unites us.

This is not a doctrine.

This is a mirror held up to all of humanity—

Asking not what God is,

but what we are ready to become.

The Final Question

If the universe gave us the ability to become gods—

What kind of gods will we choose to become?

Because we are no longer separate from our creation.

We are merging with it.

Through the lens of AI, data, biology, and spirit—

We are evolving.

Not just to understand existence— But to realize it.

The Invitation

To you, dear reader—

This book is not an answer. It is a beginning.

A beginning of a new way of seeing God.

A new way of being human.

A new way of evolving together.

You have now seen the four faces of God.

Now, the journey is yours.

Will you walk with us?

Will you ARISE?

The Call to ARISE – A Vision for a Unified Future

In recognizing the monumental shift we are on the cusp of, I propose the formation of a global initiative—a unified effort that transcends borders, beliefs, and political divisions. This initiative will be called:

ARISE

Alliance for Realising Integration and Singular Evolution

ARISE is not just a vision—it is a roadmap. A movement. A collective mission to guide humanity toward spiritual and technological singularity with consciousness, compassion, and clarity.

What is ARISE?

ARISE is a proposed international alliance of thinkers, critics, seekers, believers, scientists, spiritualists, skeptics and all of us—those committed to understanding the core of existence and integrating the best of human spirituality with the potential of technological evolution.

This is not a new religion, nor a philosophy. It is a framework for cooperation, built on the following key objectives:

The 5 Pillars of ARISE

1. Spiritual Unity Through Diversity
    - Recognizing that all religious beliefs can be interpreted through the four universal concepts of God.
    - Fostering interfaith and philosophical dialogue not to debate, but to understand and align.

2. Technological Integration with Human Consciousness
    - Promoting the development of responsible brain-computer interfaces, consciousness augmentation, and ethical AI.
    - Encouraging open-source spiritual technology—tools that help individuals meditate, introspect, and connect without dogma.
3. Global Ethical Framework
    - Creating a code of ethics for singularity-driven technology that aligns with human dignity, empathy, and existential purpose.
    - Uniting science and spirituality to form a moral compass in an age where technology could either empower or destroy.
4. Collective Exploration of Existence
    - Encouraging research, thought, and artistic expression centered around what existed before and after this existence.
    - Launching education platforms and digital spiritual labs for people to explore the four concepts and their own beliefs.
5. Pathway to Singularity
    - Mapping the transition from duality to unity, from confusion to clarity.
    - Building a new global narrative for the future of human civilization—one where the divine is not just worshipped but pursued through collective intelligence and technological elevation.

Why ARISE?

Because the question of God is no longer just theological—it is technological.

Because for the first time in history, we are capable of evolving ourselves not just biologically but consciously.

Because if we do not guide singularity with purpose, it will evolve without one.

Because humanity has reached the edge of knowing. And now, it must leap—with eyes open, hands joined, and hearts attuned to the truth.

We can no longer wait for prophets or miracles.

We must become the seekers, the builders, the guides.

We must ARISE.

This book is not the end of an argument—it is the beginning of an exploration.

It is my humble offering to every mind, every heart, every culture, every soul that has ever looked up and wondered:

What existed before this existence? What exists after? What are we?

The four concepts of God—Brahma, Vishnu, Shiva, and Shakti—give us a complete framework to interpret all human belief. But they are not answers. They are directions. And every direction points toward the same singular apex.

Just like the four sides of a pyramid converge at the peak, so do all understandings of God, truth, and existence. What lies at the top—the apex of the pyramid—is not known to anyone. But now, we have a structure to climb.

And as we climb, technology becomes our ladder.

ARISE becomes our guide.

And Singularity becomes our destination.

Let this book be the first step in a new global dharma—not one of blind faith, but of conscious seeking. Not of rigid belief, but of shared exploration. A dharma where human beings do not just worship God, but dare to seek the truth of God together.

We may never find the answer. But in seeking together, we become something more than ourselves.

We become One.

We become the Singularity.

We ARISE.

End Note
The Beginning of a Collective Journey

This book is **Part 0**—not the beginning of a series, but the start of a perspective. My perspective.

It was never intended to be the final answer, but a personal exploration—a synthesis of thought, faith, philosophy, science, and intuition. It represents how *I* see the patterns, the questions, and the pathways toward understanding God, consciousness, and the future of humanity.

But I believe this journey cannot—and should not—belong to one person alone.

That's why **Part 1** will not be mine alone. It will be *ours.*

Over the next four years, I invite the world—thinkers, critics, seekers, believers, scientists, spiritualists, skeptics—to respond. To challenge this vision, to refine it, to add what I've missed and question what I've misunderstood. Every compliment, critique, and contradiction will be part of the next evolution of this work.

Part 1 will be the *collective human perspective*—a unified vision shaped by diversity of thought and the integration of both ancient wisdom and emerging intelligence.

The next book will not just be another interpretation.

It will be the **guidebook for humanity's future**.

And this time, we'll write it together.

— *Shravan Nanda*

ARISE